# Calling
## &
# Character

# Calling & Character

## Virtues
## of the Ordained Life

## William H. Willimon

ABINGDON PRESS
NASHVILLE

CALLING AND CHARACTER:
VIRTUES OF THE ORDAINED LIFE

*This book is printed on recycled, acid-free paper.*

Library of Congress Cataloging-in-Publication Data

Willimon, William H.
   Calling & character : virtues of the ordained life / William H. Willimon.
      p. cm.
   Includes bibliographical references (p.  ) and indexes.
   ISBN 0-687-09033-4 (alk. paper)
   1. Clergy—Professional ethics.   I. Title: Calling and character.   II. Title.

BV4011.5 W55 2000
253'.2—dc21

00-058264

Scripture quotations, unless otherwise indicated, are from the New Revised Standard Version Bible, copyright © 1989, by the Division of Christian Education of the National Council of the Churches of Christ in the United States of America.

Scripture quotations marked AT are the author's translation.

The Code of Ethics for Clergy and Other Church Professionals, quoted in the appendix, is used by permission of the Council of National Capital Presbytery.

Prayers from the introduction, chapter 1, and chapter 5 are taken from *The United Methodist Book of Worship* © 1992 by The United Methodist Publishing House and are used by permission.

02 03 04 05 06 07 08 09—10 9 8 7 6 5

MANUFACTURED IN THE UNITED STATES OF AMERICA

# Contents

103206

For

Brenda and Keith Brodie

Gracious God,

give to these your servants the grace and power they need

to serve you in this ministry,

so that your people may be strengthened

and your name glorified in all the world.

Make them faithful pastors, patient teachers, and wise

counselors.

Enable them to serve without reproach,

to proclaim the gospel of salvation,

to administer the Sacraments of the new covenant,

to order the life of the Church,

and to offer with all your people

spiritual sacrifices acceptable to you;

through Jesus Christ our Lord,

who lives and reigns with you,

in the unity of the Holy Spirit,

one God, now and for ever. **Amen.**[1]

# Introduction

Why clergy ethics? Why not simply Christian ethics? It is a fair question. Most of the ethical dilemmas of clergy are not too different from those of all Christians. We clergy ought not to flatter ourselves, as if our clerical vocation somehow placed a greater burden upon our backs than the challenge that taking up the cross and following Jesus holds for any disciple. It is not easy for any of us to be baptized. Yet some of the ethical dilemmas faced by the church today really do seem peculiar to clergy. This book is about those challenges.

Frankly, there is little explicit mention in the New Testament about the ethics of Christian leadership, except for a few snippets in the Gospels and a couple of the Pastoral Epistles. Rarely does the New Testament take time to deal with leadership issues in the church, certainly not as much space as is expended in the Old Testament's detailed treatment of the moral and physical attributes of priests for the Temple. Great mischief was worked in the ministry of the church when, during the Middle Ages, Christian theologians began reading Old

Testament requirements for priests back toward Christian clergy. Christian clergy became a special class of Christians laid over the lowly laity, and were considered especially pure people who had unique chrisms, the sacerdotal *cleros* in distinction from the ordinary *laos*.

There is widespread agreement that clergy are "special" among all Christians. How are they special? That is the question. We cannot know how clergy ought to live until we first are clear what clergy are for.

Clergy are special, not because they have received some unique grace not to be had by other Christians, nor because clergy know many things that the lowly laity do not. Rather, clergy are significant as officials of the church, as those who have had their lives yoked to the body of Christ in a way that makes their vocation uniquely linked to the care of the Christian community. My starting point for thinking about the ordained leadership of the church is baptism, the ministry of all Christians for which ordained, pastoral ministry is but a species of a broader genus called the ministry of the baptized. We clergy have significance, we ought to be praised or blamed, on the basis of what ought to happen among the baptized.

Of course, the Christian Scriptures appear not to do ethics very often—ethics as lists of right behaviors, codes of conduct, moral dilemmas. Explicit modes of ethical deliberation are generally not the way the Scriptures get at the Socratic question, "How then should we live?" Scripture tends not to be systematic, as we think of systems of thought; it tends not to begin with certain general good principles, moving then to specific behaviors required by adherence to those principles, as is often taught.

Most of the ethics in Scripture is by implication, derivative of the narrative of our salvation, derivative of Scripture's determination to help us to worship the true and living God.[2] The Acts of the Apostles is, by my reckoning, a great early Christian treatise on Christian ministry, but Acts hardly ever turns away from its drama to give ethical admonition. Rather, all ethics is by implication, through imaginative, dynamic analogy, by creative inference from the models for ministry of people like Paul, Barnabas, Peter, and Tabitha. As Stanley Hauerwas has said, "The lives of the saints are the hermeneutical key to Scripture."[3] The saints are also our key to the performance, the embodiment, and enactment of Scripture, otherwise known as Christian ethics. That is one reason why I end many of the sections in this book with concrete examples of clergy who either demonstrated or violated Christian ethics in their ministry.

This book is concerned not with a method of ethical deliberation for pastors, not with the solution of various ethical quandaries of clergy, but rather with the basic question, Who ought clergy be? and then by implication, What ought clergy to do? It is the character of clergy that is our main concern. Christian ethics is both training in who to be, or in how to see, as well as instruction in what we ought to do. Furthermore, Christian ethics is church ethics. It is not heroic, not meant as some impossible ideal. Clergy, like all baptized Christians, are expected to witness to the death and resurrection of Jesus by the way that we live. In this sense, when it comes to Christian ethical dilemmas, clergy are not special.

However, from among the baptized, the church has found it helpful to call some to lead the church, to care for congregations, to preach the Word and to administer the sacraments, to worry about what makes the church, church, in a way that is helpful to all members of the body of Christ as they live out their vocations. Christians so designated—ordained, placed under orders by the church—are called pastors, priests, or clergy. This book seeks to highlight those ethical challenges that are peculiar to clergy, the morality and virtues that adhere to the practice of Christian leadership today and the way in which clerical character informs those challenges. It is based upon my conviction that our clergy problem is more a matter of morale than morals.

Since the Middle Ages, the study of Christian ethics has been mostly about theory and theology. Moral theology has been concerned with practice. Ethics is about affirmations, beliefs, commitments, and character while morals is about action, behavior, and casuistry. Or to put it another way, ethics is about our reasons for doing the things we do and morality is what we do or ought not to do.

In a sense, concern over character is interested both in ethics and morality, particularly as these matters impinge upon and demonstrate the shape of a particular moral agent who is deciding, acting, and avoiding morality. Ethics is both about making normative judgments concerning right behavior in the light of the gospel and about analysis of various moral dilemmas faced by clergy. This book begins with an overriding concern for the nature of clergy character, then examines some of the ways in which the practice of ministry raises questions about how our Christian commitments ought to be exemplified by the lives we lead as ministers.[4] There is a certain prejudicing in favor of "being over doing" in any character ethics. But I consider that character ethics implies a complementary arrangement in which our moral quandaries and dilemmas are most interesting as they relate to the sort of persons we are or hope to be, while our characters set our quandaries and dilemmas in their proper context. In short, there is no way to divorce the question, "What ought I to do?" from "Who do I hope to be?" or vice versa.

I do not believe that clergy character is in worse shape today than at other times in church history. Infidelity has always been a problem, even with Jesus' first inner circle of disciples. Once, when lamenting some of the more notable moral lapses of my fellow clergy in the present age, I said in the hearing of a retired pastor, a man whom I greatly admire, "There once was a time when clergy had a sense of being morally elite. Not anymore. Today's clergy are a sad commentary on the state of the church."

He gently reminded me that the saintly period toward which I looked so wistfully, the time of much of his early ministry and my boyhood, was also a time of racial segregation in the South when few clergy dared to challenge so vast a social evil.

Jesus questioned whether or not we were able to "be baptized with the baptism that I am baptized with?" (Mark 10:38). There is much failure in the ordained ministry today—and always has been. Therefore, one of the challenges of clergy ethics is to name our failures rightly. The cross itself seemed to the world like Jesus' great failure. We learned to name this as God's great victory. We Christians must constantly critique what the world regards as success and what the world thinks of as failure. Just last Sunday I was given by the lectionary a most troublesome text to preach. The congregational consensus seemed to be that I preached it well enough. I received an unusual number of compliments at the end of service (six, to be exact). They noted how engaging my sermon was, how helpful I was in explaining to their satisfaction what had long been for them a difficult biblical passage. More than one person appreciated my humor.

From the serene vantage point of Monday, however, I now consider that sermon to be a moral failure. The reasons for this reassessment would require an explication of the peculiar ethical demands for faithful Christian preaching. I am called to preach Christ and him crucified, not to make his gospel more accessible than he himself managed to make it. Chrysostom, to whom I am heavily indebted for my exposition of clerical character (as you will soon see), said that a preacher must "despise praise." At the conclusion of one of his sermons in Constantinople, when the congregation broke into enthusiastic applause, Chrysostom turned on the congregation and mocked them for applauding what they had no intention of taking to heart, derided them as scoundrels unworthy of the gospel, and announced that all applause would hereafter be forbidden in this church. This announcement brought down the house with applause.[5]

I therefore hope that it will be evident in the succeeding pages that I write as a pastor who is not immune from any of the temptations and many of the failings of character that I describe. I write as a pastor, to women and men who have been called to share in this high, difficult calling.[6] I do not write as an ethical "expert," if there can be such an animal. Time and again throughout this book, when dealing with some specific ethical dilemma, I ought to be honest enough to say with Paul, "I have no command of the Lord, but I give my opinion as one who by the Lord's mercy is trustworthy" (1 Cor. 7:25). The church has not seen fit to place me in a position to judge or to discipline my fellow clergy. My only goal is to persuade you that while God has called us clergy to a work that is difficult, it is not impossible, and that we ought not to waste the grace of God by shirking our high calling.

Most of all, I write as one who, even after nearly three decades of ministry, is almost daily delighted that, of all the people who could have been chosen by God and the church to lead, God and the church chose me.

William H. Willimon
Monday after the Eighteenth Sunday after Pentecost

# CHAPTER ONE

## *Vocation*

The Acts of the Apostles begins in great drama. The risen Christ ascends to heaven (1:6-11). Yet scarcely six verses later, Peter stands up and admits that Judas, who was "numbered among us and allotted his share in this ministry" (1:17) had collaborated with those who arrested Jesus. If one is looking for betrayers of Christ, one need look no farther than Jesus' own disciples.

Then there is an election of a replacement apostle by asking, "Lord . . . show us which one of these two you have chosen to take the place in this ministry" (1:24-25). Once lots are cast, Matthias is added to the eleven.

After the excitement of the resurrection and ascension, this seems a pedestrian way to begin the story of the church. The response to the ascension of Christ is a church meeting where a vote is taken. Yet I read this as Luke's way of asserting that leadership is not optional in the church. There is no church without apostleship, without leaders who are chosen on the basis of qualifications (1:21-22) and by divine choice (1:24). Church leaders come both from the "bottom up"—from the ranks of those whom the community chooses to lead—

and from the "top down"—as gifts of a gracious God who does not leave the church bereft of the guidance it needs to fulfill its mission. Leaders are not some later bureaucratic invention foisted upon a once democratic and egalitarian church by power-hungry authoritarians. The church is, in this sense, inherently hierarchical, dependent upon the leadership of those who are commissioned by the Holy Spirit working through the church, for its fidelity.

The Matthias episode at the beginning of Acts reminds us that ministry begins in the heart of God, in God's relentless determination to have a people, a family. In order to have a family, a holy nation, a kingdom of priests able to declare the wonderful deeds of the One who brought us from darkness to light (1 Pet. 2:9), there must be leaders.

So, to the murderer Moses, hiding out in Midian, working for his father-in-law, God appears in a burning bush saying, "I have heard the cry of my people. I am going to liberate them. And guess who is going to help me?"

Moses protests. He is not good at public speaking. He has baggage. Yet Moses finds what succeeding generations found. Once comes the call to service, it is futile to wrestle with God. Once God has got in God's mind that someone is a leader, one might as well relent with a deferential, "Here am I, send me."

Ministry is therefore something that God does through the church before it is anything we do. Our significance, as leaders, is responsive. We are here, in leadership of God's people, because we have responded to a summons, because we were sought, called, sent, commissioned by one greater than ourselves that our lives might be expended in work more significant than ourselves. It all begins in vocation. As Calvin noted, God calls, but the church must also call. We believe that in this twofold call to ministry is God's very voice calling leadership to the church that the church could not have through its own efforts. Vocation is just one of God's gracious gifts to the church so that the church might be the church.

## SERVICE

That which we call "ministry" is, in the New Testament, *diakonia,* from which we get the Greek word for "service." This is Paul's favorite title for Christian leaders (1 Cor. 12:4-30). Significantly, it is the same word that is the root for "butler" and "waiter." We pastors sometimes overlook how odd it is that the church designates its leaders by so mundane and lowly a term. No pastor rises much higher than the role of a butler waiting on table. Yet, in the curious topsy-turvy ethics of the Kingdom, this is as high as anyone rises, a servant of those seated at the Lord's Table.

So we begin our exploration of clergy ethics by inquiry into clergy identity. Every "ought" arises from an "is," all imperatives ("you should") are derived from indicatives ("you are"). We cannot judge how pastors ought to behave unless we first inquire into who pastors are. And to know who pastors are, we ought to know what pastors are for.[1]

That the table being waited upon is the Lord's and those gathered are none other than the body of Christ makes all the difference for the *diakonoi.* Jesus, the one who modeled leadership with a basin and towel, was at some pains to admonish his followers that they ought not to behave like a bunch of power-grubbing "gentiles." "It is not so among you; but whoever wishes to become great among you must be your servant *(diakonos),* and whoever wishes to be first among you must be slave *(doulos)* of all" (Mark 10:43-44).[2] The mention here of ser-

vant and slave obviously indicates we are dealing with a
very peculiar definition of leadership.

Later, when Ephesians speaks of the church's leaders
as "apostles," "prophets," "evangelists," "pastors and
teachers," it says that all of these share the servile function to "equip the saints for the work of ministry *(diakonia)*" (Eph. 4:11-12). These ministers have as their
purpose to "equip the saints," that is, the whole church,
so that the church can be about "the work of ministry."
The significance of pastors is derived from what needs to
happen among the ministers, that is *church*. As Luther
later stressed, all Christians, by virtue of our baptism,
are called to be evangelists, teachers, preachers, and
healers. But for the sake of good order, the church has
found it helpful to designate some from among the baptized to equip and to encourage the evangelists, teachers,
preachers, and healers. These equippers of the saints are
called "pastors." Even 1 Timothy's high view of bishops
is based upon their function to "take care of God's
church" (3:5).

Reading between the lines in Acts or the Pastoral
Epistles, we know that there have always been moral
challenges for the church's leaders. The Christ of the
Fourth Gospel warns of unworthy shepherds who care
little for the sheep, who are no more than thieves and
robbers (John 10:1-10). I have always loved the way the
Common Lectionary places this text just after Easter
(Easter 4 A), just before Pentecost, as if to warn the
church that, though resurrection may be true and though
the gift of the Holy Spirit is given to the church, don't be
surprised when some shepherd of this resurrected,
Spirit-empowered flock lacks the character to be left
alone with the sheep.

In contrast to most of the New Testament, 1 Timothy
makes explicit mention of the moral qualities of
Christian leaders:

> Now a bishop [Greek: *episkopos;* sometimes translated as *overseer*] must be above reproach, married only once, temperate, sensible, respectable, hospitable, an apt teacher, not a drunkard, not violent but gentle, not quarrelsome, and not a lover of money (1 Tim. 3:2-3)

First Timothy has no qualms about linking a pastor's public, congregational role with the pastor's responsibility toward marriage and family. Clearly, pastors are to be role models for the church, without separation between public and private, social and personal behavior. When listing the moral duties of pastors, 1 Timothy contrasts "sound teaching" (4:6) with assorted immoral conduct (1:8-11). A pastor who is an unfaithful teacher, indifferent to sound doctrine, is considered by this epistle to be among the greatest of moral failures. In all things, it is clear that Christian leaders are visibly to represent a manner of life and a style of leadership in marked contrast to that of the world.

This countercultural, peculiar quality of church leadership was sorely tested in events that occurred during the fourth century. Imperial persecution suddenly ceased. Christian clergy, once the leaders of a subversive, sometimes persecuted and often just ignored sect on the fringes of the Empire, were about to become representatives of the state. The earlier tensive relationship between church and culture was relaxed. There were some, it was said, who sought ecclesiastical office (note that leadership is becoming an "office" in addition to a vocation) for economic or political advancement.

Perhaps it was this cultural context that gave rise to one of the greatest expositions on the Christian ministry, John Chrysostom's *Treatise Concerning the Christian Priesthood* (c. 386).[3] The occasion for Chrysostom's writing on ministry was his being pressured by friends to become a bishop. In giving all the reasons why he was not, at this time, worthy of the episcopate, Chrysostom offers us a wonderful basis for thinking about the character required to be a pastor.

Although he had come from a highly placed Roman administrative family, Chrysostom had become a monk. His main reason why he thought that he should not leave the hermetic life and enter into the public push-and-pull of the episcopacy was his great respect for those who are able to remain holy even while engaged in the demanding work of building up the church. Monks had it easier, said Chrysostom.

In those days, the expectation was that one became a bishop, not at the end of an exhausting and degrading political campaign, but rather as a result of a responsibility bestowed by the church. The episcopacy was viewed not as an office that was sought with savviness, but rather as a burden that was assumed with reluctance.

Chrysostom believes that the peculiar nature of the pastorate, caring for the community of faith, makes the priesthood a particularly demanding vocation. It is the politics of it all that makes the pastoral ministry so difficult. A bishop has somehow got to be a pleasing bundle of polarities, "dignified yet modest, awe-inspiring yet kindly, masterful yet accessible, impartial yet courteous, humble yet not servile, vehement yet gentle."[4] The pastoral overseer must hold all these conflicting qualities together in his person yet will only one thing, "the edification of the Church." Politically, a good priest must have "a thousand eyes in every direction."

In toiling long and hard on his sermons, the priest must at the same time be utterly indifferent to the praise of his hearers, says Chrysostom. He exemplified such homiletical courage when, as Bishop of Constantinople (he finally relented to the entreaties of the church and became a bishop in 397), Chrysostom roundly rebuked the Empress Eudoxia as nothing but a Jezebel, preaching in a fashion that earned him exile not once but twice.

While Chrysostom goes so far as to say that priests are superior even to the angels, because priests have been given the power to loose the bonds of sin, he notes that it is the peculiar burden of the priest to be judged by his parish as if he were an angel and not of the same frail stuff as the rest of humanity. If there is even the slightest bit of stubble in the building of his life, congregational envy, vexed parishioners, or rival clerics will seize upon such moral failings in the priest and the whole edifice will be "scorched and utterly blackened by the smoke."

Ambrose of Milan (c. 339–397) was the Western counterpart to Chrysostom. In the very same year that Chrysostom wrote his *Treatise Concerning the Christian Priesthood*, Ambrose wrote *On the Duties of Ministers* (386). It is interesting that both of these church fathers, at different ends of the Empire, felt the need to comment on clerical ethical problems at the same time. Utilizing the *De officiis* of Cicero, Ambrose draws up a list of desirable virtues for clergy, augmenting Cicero's book of virtues for pagan governmental officials and applying them to Christian clergy, putting a sort of Christian veneer upon pagan ethics.

My approach is indebted more to Chrysostom, who begins his consideration of the virtues of priests by considering first their vocation. What pastors do is a function of who pastors are. The great ethical danger for clergy is not that we might "burn out," to use a metaphor that is popular in our time, not that we might lose the energy required to do ministry. Our danger is that we might "black out," that is lose consciousness of why we are here and who we are called to be for Christ and his church. It is easy, amid the great demands of the pastoral ministry, to lose sight of that vision that once called us into being as pastors. Periodic refurbishment of our vision is needed. Take this book as an attempt to address the ethical crises of pastors by renourishing the vision by which pastors are called.

Vocation to service, in my experience, is one of the main sources of motivation for constancy in ministry. There are many times in the pastoral ministry when we see no visible results of our efforts, have no sense that people are getting better because of our work among them, have little proof of our effectiveness as priests. In those moments, our only hope is to cling to our vocation, to adhere to the sense that God has called us, rather than we ourselves, that God has a plan and purpose for how our meager efforts fit into God's larger scheme of things. God's vocation is the only ultimate validation of our ministry.

Years ago a friend of mine, Robert Wilson, distinguished sociologist of religion, conducted a survey among some clergy of the Episcopal Church and clergy of the Church of God (Anderson, Indiana), inquiring into their happiness and satisfaction with ministry. The Episcopal clergy had a much larger amount of financial compensation for their work, lived in larger, better-equipped parsonages, and had more generous pension programs than the clergy in the Church of God. Yet the Episcopal priests were also far less happy and content in their ministry. Many of them showed low morale and deep unhappiness, particularly when compared to the Church of God ministers. Why?

Wilson said that he thought part of the problem lay in differences between how each group conceived of its ministry. The Episcopalians, according to Wilson's interviews, saw themselves as "professionals"—well educated and trained, though poorly employed and compensated, professionals. The Church of God clergy, on the other hand, saw themselves as called, willed by God to work in the Church of God; people sent on a mission.

"You can't pay people to do the things that ministers routinely must do," said Wilson. "They need to think God has called them, or ministry is miserable."

All historic rites of ordination include a general examination of candidates for ministry. It is interesting that ordination begins with so strong an ethical examination and injunction. Ministry is apparently a vocation that is against our natural, cultural inclinations. Therefore the church enjoins us to remember that we are called, that ministry is God's idea before it is ours, to seek God's help to be faithful to God's calling.

Recently, a group of Christian and Jewish ethicists and theologians issued a formidable group of essays collected in *Clergy Ethics in a Changing Society.*[5] As a whole, the volume is a testimonial to the frequently heard charge that today's clergy are confused about who they are and what they are supposed to be doing. Generally speaking, clergy ethics is described in these essays as a personality disorder among pastors, with little reference to church, Scripture, or tradition. Exceptions are the essays by William May on "Images of the Minister" and Rebecca S. Chopp on "Liberating Ministry." Chopp's essay is interesting mainly because she is a liberation theologian and her essay therefore has a point of view and some unashamed commitments that give her interesting opinions about our allegedly "changing society." I do wonder, though, if an emphasis upon "liberation" as a guiding metaphor is inappropriate to the practice of Christian ministry. The notion of "liberation" as a basis for ethics tends to build upon the Western notion that we are most fully ourselves when we have the fewest obligations to others.

None of the essays in *Clergy Ethics* refers to the rites of ordination, a curious fact since, if one wants to know who clergy are and what they are supposed to be doing, one might consult those ecclesial statements made to and about clergy when the church ordained them. The lack of reference to rites of ordination leads to a depiction of clergy ethics as essentially self-derived, something constructed by pastors themselves in their attempt to be moral. Martin Marty's title for his essay typifies the problem: "Ministers on Their Own."

My friend Stanley Hauerwas was recently asked at a clergy conference about the moral confusion of contemporary clergy. Hauerwas said something to the effect that, "You have these people who get out of seminary thinking that their job is to 'help people.' That's where the adultery begins."

What?

"You have these clergy," he continued, "who have no better reason for being in ministry than to 'meet people's needs.' So little Johnny needs picking up after school. And Johnny's mother, since she is working, calls the pastor, who has nothing else better to do, and asks him to pick up little Johnny. And the pastor thinks, 'Well, I'm here to help people.' So he goes and picks up little Johnny. Before long the pastor meets a parishioner who is lonely and needs love and then, when caught in the act of adultery, his defense is that he is an extremely caring pastor."[6]

I recalled what I thought to be, at the time, a rather silly article in *The Christian Century* by a pastoral care professor entitled, "Clergy Adultery as Role Confusion." I wondered, what about "Clergy Adultery as *Sin*"? But the more I have thought about it, the more I see that professor's point. In a culture of omnivorous need, all-consuming narcissism, clergy who have no more compelling motive for their ministry than "meeting people's needs" are dangerous to themselves and to a church that lacks a clear sense of who it is.

Lacking a strong sense of their peculiar communal vocation, contemporary clergy have no means of resisting the tendency to wallow in the same psychotherapeutic mire as our people—meeting our needs, looking out for number one, if it feels good do it, the relentless scanning and feeding of the ego.

We must be called, recalled to the joy of being grasped by something greater than ourselves, namely our vocation to speak and to enact the Word of God among God's people. Morality is a matter not of being unattached to any external determination, free to think and act on the basis of our personal feelings of what's right. Contrary to the beliefs of liberalism, morality comes as a gracious by-product of being attached to something greater than ourselves, of being owned, claimed, commandeered for larger purposes.

My own ministerial moral ineptitude was made vividly manifest to me a few years ago. Shortly after the war with Iraq, I received a note from one of the older members of my congregation, a note written on light-blue stationery, neatly folded, and written in a frail, but still lovely hand.

"Have you preached on this particular episode, have you mentioned it in one of your recent sermons? Now that I can't get out and about, I listen on the radio to your sermons, but I do not recall your having mentioned this."

She was referring to a newspaper story (the clipping neatly folded within the same light-blue envelope) about how American troops had buried alive as many as six hundred Iraqi soldiers in their trenches during a battle. "By the time we got there," one soldier was quoted as saying, "all that was left was hands and arms sticking up out of the sand."

"What does this do to the moral character of our nation?" she asked, in graceful, antique handwriting on the blue notepaper. "I grieve for the soul of our country. Where is the moral voice of our clergy in these matters?"

Her words stunned me into renewal of my vocation. The problem was not that I had been too timid in my preaching, too fixated in pop psychology to notice the ethical cataclysm taking place outside our sanctuary, too

absorbed with the purely personal problems of my affluent congregation—although all these statements are
true. My problem was not first a matter of morality. It
was a problem of vocation, a need to be authorized by
something more important than my own needs, or even
my assessment of the needs of my congregation.

I recalled a wonderful comment once made by a
scholar, something said to us preachers like, "If you are
a coward by nature, don't worry. You don't have to be
courageous to be a preacher. All you have to do is to get
down behind the text. You can say, 'This is not necessarily me saying this—but I do think the text says it.'"

We can hunker down behind the text! By remaining
disjoined from service to the text, and having no vocation to serve the Word, all I can do is to serve the congregational status quo, run pastoral errands for the
world as it is rather than let God use me to create a new
world. And that is not only no fun, it's also immoral.

In a culture that has lost its moral compass (what we
did in Iraq for the oil companies has its counterpart in
what we are doing to one another in bedrooms), that
parishioner's note on blue stationery called me back to
the ethical significance of preaching.

I urge all seminarians to read what is, in my opinion,
one of the best novels of the late nineteenth century, certainly one of the best novels on the peculiar moral dilemmas of clergy. It is Harold Frederic's *Damnation of Theron
Ware* (1896). A young Methodist preacher is called to
preach, but called more so to advance socially through
his preaching. Stifled by the confines of petty morality in
the midwestern town where he serves, the Reverend
Ware longs for a larger stage on which to display his
homiletical talents. His best friends—the urbane Father
Forbes of the nearby Catholic church, Dr. Ledsmar, the
town's one social Darwinian, and Celia Madden, a
wealthy connoisseur of the arts—represent all that Ware

wants to be in life. The more these friends urge him to sample a social life out of his present reach, the less he regards his own ministerial vocation. His vocation becomes a career, a path up the social ladder through the flattering, eloquent art of his preaching.

Adultery (what is there about us clergy that makes us so susceptible to this temptation?) is not far behind. When Ware finally confesses his love for Celia, she announces to him that his presumed "improvement" has only served to render a once adequate pastor into a first-class bore. Ware eventually leaves the ministry, a victim of his own craving for status and recognition.

Of course, Ware's descent to the level of a rather common adulterer has nothing to do with his inability to meet his personal needs or with his being out of touch with his feelings as a man. His descent is related to his inability to be attached to his vocation as a preacher. When that vocation becomes a mere means to an end, flaws in the preacher's character that may have been overcome by the preacher's attachment to his calling are magnified, and the same banal temptations that afflict any other member of this society are almost irresistible.

At times our pastoral vocation conflicts and collides with our other callings, most frequently with our marital vocation. One can easily understand why the Catholic tradition asserted that the two were incompatible and therefore demanded that its priests be celibate. As Robert Jenson says, marital vows and ordination vows are "totalitarian in the lives of those who enter them." Perhaps, as Jenson goes on to say, Luther was right to insist that these two totalitarian vocations be inter-woven, backed up by a new social creation that was peculiar enough and strong enough to sustain them, namely the pastoral family.[7]

Might it be claimed that the vocations of ordination and marriage can be complementary rather than merely conflicted? Both vocations are best seen as forms of Christian service, as two ways of living out our baptism in service to others. As a pastor, many marriages in my congregation are collapsing under their own weight. They are failing, not because people expect too little from marriage but because people expect too much. They have no more significant reason to be married than simply being married.

Marriage, from my experience of it, tends to be symbiotic. It feeds off of experiences outside the marriage. It can be a boon to marriage for the marriage to be seen as complementary to and supportive of another demanding and invigorating vocation, namely the expenditure of a life in service to Christ and the church. Marriage may be the sort of vocation that cannot stand alone, that needs a network of more important commitments to make the commitment of exclusive, lifelong fidelity work.

Because I conceive of clergy ethics as something that is imposed upon clergy by their vocation, I believe that clergy seeking a moral basis for their ministry would do well to attend more closely to the ordinal of the church. When someone is ordained as a leader of the church, hands are laid upon the person's head as a gesture of giving and receiving power and of vesting with the community's authority, which should be the basis of anything we say about clergy ethics. Listen to these words from the United Methodist rite of ordination:

> My *sisters and brothers,*
>     all Christians are called through baptism
>     to share in Christ's ministry of love and service.
> This ministry is empowered by God's Holy Spirit
>     for the redemption of the human family and the whole
> of creation.
>
> You have been called,
>     by the spirit of God working in you,
>     to a representative ministry within the people of God.

Christ's body, the Church,
   now confirms your calling through consecration or
ordination.

You are to lead the people of God in worship and prayer,
   and to nurture, teach, and encourage them
   from the riches of God's grace.
You are to exemplify Christ's servanthood;
   to build up the people of God
   in their obedience to Christ's mission in the world,
   and to seek justice, peace, and salvation for all people.

As representative ministers in the church,
   you are to be coworkers with the bishops,
   deacons, diaconal ministers, and elders.
It is your task to proclaim by word and deed the gospel
of Jesus Christ,
   to lead persons to faith in Jesus Christ,
   and to conform your life in accordance with the gospel.

Remember that you are called
   to serve rather than to be served,
   to proclaim the faith of the Church and no other,
   to look after the concerns of Christ above all.

So that we may know that you believe yourselves
   to be called by God
   and that you profess the Christian faith,
we ask you:

Do you trust that you are called by God
   to the life and work of representative ministry in the
Church?

**I do so trust.**

Do you believe in the Triune God,
   and confess Jesus Christ as your Lord and Savior?

**I do so believe and confess.**

Are you persuaded

that the scriptures of the Old and New Testaments
contain all things necessary for salvation
through faith in Jesus Christ,
and are the unique and authoritative standard
for the Church's faith and life?

**I am so persuaded, by God's grace.**

Will you be faithful in prayer,
in the reading and study of the Holy Scriptures,
and with the help of the Holy Spirit
continually rekindle the gift of God that is in you?

**I will, God being my helper.**[8]

# CHAPTER TWO

# *The Character of Clergy*

Our seminarians complain that, upon graduation from seminary, they are overwhelmed by the gap between the church that they expected and the church that they got. I am unimpressed that there is a huge gap between the theological definition of ministry and its sociological reality. As Richard Neuhaus says in the opening pages of his classic book on ministry, "there is a necessary awkwardness about Christian ministry because we are ambassadors of a 'disputed sovereignty.'"[1] That "necessary awkwardness," that persistent sense that we are representatives of a sovereign who is in contention with the reigning principalities and powers, is a major source of all ethics worthy of the name Christian. The gospel is inherently countercultural and conflictual with all cultures, including the very first culture in which it made its way, and including the culture called the church that seeks to domesticate the gospel. Service to that gospel is bound to be countercultural because the gospel itself engenders a "culture" with its own distinctive symbols, language, myths, and ethic. The great challenge of the Christian ministry, since its inception, is how to work within a given culture without being subsumed by it.[2] It takes great character to do so. The other great challenge is that, by nature, none of us is born well-suited to the ministry. *Diakonia* is against our natural inclination. Therefore, pastoral ethics is also about formation.

One of the burdens of the pastoral ministry today is that pastors, realizing that they have few skills or little esoteric knowledge not readily available to all Christians, attempt to be extraordinarily nice. The pastor is the Christian who is incredibly warm, affirming, understanding, patient, and popular. This is a curious reworking of the older image of the pastor as the vicarious saint of the congregation, the person who is paid to be more saintly than all the other saints. Pastors can be preserved from this perversion only by cultivating the awareness that ministry receives its significance from what needs to happen in the church, that its power proceeds, not from the pleasing personality of the pastor, but from the authorization of God through the church.

## CLERGY CHARACTERS

Ministry is not a "profession," as the term is often used. While it is important for ministers to be competent and proficient in the tasks of ministry, the deep difficulty suffered by two corrupted professions today—law and medicine—warns us that a profession was first a moral matter. A profession is a matter of someone being formed into an exemplary person by being attached to a noble body of belief like jurisprudence or care of the sick. We have degraded "professionals" by making them primarily people who know something that the rest of us do not, rather than being people who the rest of us are not.

In one important sense clergy are members of a profession. The designation "professional" was first applied to clergy. A professional was first a person who had something to profess, some body of knowledge, an allegiance to some notion of the higher good, some attachment to goods and goals more significant than the self. One of the deep problems with the two "professions" of medicine and law today is that doctors and lawyers often appear to have nothing more significant to "profess" than their patients and clients. Medicine and law think that their primary purpose is to serve consumers, rather than public health or jurisprudence. Pastors profess God. Pastors are accountable to God; the test of their work is someone more significant even than their parishioners. In all their pastoral work, pastors are professing faith in God, not in the supposed needs of their people.[3]

Ministry is not merely a profession, not only because one cannot pay pastors to do many of the things they routinely do, but also because ministry is a vocation. Ministers are more than those who are credentialed and validated by the approval of their fellow members of their profession. Ministers must be called. True, Christians believe that all occupations ought to answer to the vocational question, namely, How is this work an extension of your Christian discipleship? For clergy, this sense of vocational responsibility is crucial due to the peculiar demands upon ministers.

Pastors, like doctors and lawyers, deal with matters that really matter, like sex, marriage, death, and salvation.[4] Because so much is at stake in these matters, and because the issues involved are rarely clear-cut, not only is wise discernment required, but also good judgment, an ability to know each situation on its own, and above all, honest self-knowledge. Aristotle, on whose thought my emphasis upon character is based, stressed that good works arise from good people. In order to do good, one must gain wisdom, experience, and self-control. He noted that some of the best things we do as people occur

not because we have rationally thought through all possible alternatives, not because we have adhered to some
moral code or set of principles, but simply because we
responded out of habit, out of an ingrained, inculcated
pattern of living. Our actions were "second nature" to
us, congruent with who we are and who we hope to be.
This, said Aristotle, is ethics worthy of the name.

Even in the area of public speaking, especially there,
Aristotle sees character as an essential requirement. Of
the three artistic forms of proof that Aristotle listed as
being available to the public speaker—*logos, pathos,* and
*ethos*—Aristotle knew that *ethos,* the character of the
speaker "constitutes the most effective means of proof"
(*Rhetoric,* I, ii).[5] Cato, likewise, defined a good speech as
a good person speaking well.

While Augustine admits that it is possible, due to the
work of the Holy Spirit, that some good might come
from the preaching of a morally corrupt preacher ("men
who themselves lead unprofitable lives are sometimes
heard with profit by others"), he asserts that "they
would do good to very many more if they lived as they
preach. For there are numbers who seek an excuse for
their own evil lives in comparing the teaching with the
conduct of their instructors, and who say in their hearts,
'Why do you not do yourself what you bid me do?' and
in despising the preacher learn to despise the word that
is preached."[6]

"That's just what I would have expected her to do in
that situation," is an everyday observation of character
in a coherent, well-formed, person. Character is predis-
position toward certain conduct rather than prescrip-
tion. Of course, in considerations of character as morally
significant, it makes all the difference what the moral
agent will do, has done, and is doing. In character, a person's professed principles and values are embodied and
enacted. In fact, without such embodiment, a person's

professed "values" are uninteresting and without consequence.[7]

In his polemic against the Donatists, Augustine linked character with baptism. Just as a Roman soldier was tattooed as a sign of his membership in the Roman army *(character militiae)*, so Christians, signed with the cross in baptism, have been indelibly stamped with the cross *(character dominicus)*. This character, the cross, indelibly determines our character. Through the vicissitudes of time, and place, and changes in personality, this character persists.

The Donatists claimed that those who had been ordained by bishops who handed over the Scriptures to the governmental authorities during the times of persecution were morally incapable of officiating in the rites of the church. A baptism done by a Donatist-ordained priest was no baptism.

Augustine countered that the sacrament has an efficacy that is not solely defined by the personality of the priest. A priest who is a scoundrel and who performs a baptism is still someone who bears the character conferred through ordination. The baptism is valid, despite the personality of the priest. Furthermore, there is an indelible character conferred in ordination that transcends the personal limits of the priest. The laying on of hands with prayer makes a person different, changes that person as radically as a royal seal changes the quality of metal when it is stamped into a coin by the *signum regale*. While such talk undeniably led to an *ex opera operata* view of ministerial authority during the Middle Ages, Augustine qualified his stress upon the indelible character of clergy by noting that there is a difference between ministerial authority that is only sacramentally bestowed and that which is earned through faithful ministry.

Listen as Gregory of Nyssa (c. 376) describes what happens to the ordinand in the process of ordination:

> The same power of the word...makes the priest vener-
> able and honorable, separated....While but yesterday he
> was one of the mass, one of the people, he is suddenly
> rendered a guide, a president, a teacher of righteousness,
> an instructor in hidden mysteries, metamorphosed to the
> higher condition. *(On the Baptism of Christ)*[8]

While Augustine's argument for an ordained indelible character in the clergy had a great impact upon the doctrine of ordination in the West, some say that such a doctrine undercuts clergy ethics. Why worry about the moral character of a priest if the priest's behavior or disposition is ultimately overridden by the power of ordination?

Yet the claim that ordination makes someone different, through the actions of God and the church, can also be the very basis of clerical ethics. Pastors are those who have had hands laid upon their heads. That act signifies, effects, represents, and testifies to the bestowal of authority that is the starting point for any reflection upon right or wrong clerical action. Ordination, as the basis for who I now am, is also a great comfort to me as I go about my pastoral work.

I recall being urged by a pastoral care professor to "just share your self with your people." Fortunately, we pastors have considerably more than ourselves to share. Our people need more than just another well-intentioned person in their need. In a sermon Augustine admitted to his people that he labored under a paradox: "For you I am a bishop but with you I am a Christian." A pastor must somehow be the Christian who is ordained to lead but also never lose sight that he or she is a struggling sinner, like all Christians, in need of the grace of God. Today, in my observation, we pastors struggle more with the first part of that equation. We are Christians who bear the need of our people for a priest. They need a priest, someone to mediate between them and God.

Ordination is a sign of that formation of character. It is great grace to be able, in our difficult times in ministry, to fall back upon that authorization, that empowerment that is beyond ourselves. The authorization of God and the church, symbolized by the laying on of hands, is our strength in our weakness. Ordination makes us more than we could have been if we had been left to our good intentions and well-meaning devices.

When discussing the virtues necessary for a good teacher, Aristotle stressed self-knowledge as the most important. Whenever someone is in a position of power over another person, such as a teacher who rules over a student, the person in power must be deeply aware of his or her inclinations, dispositions, strengths, and weaknesses or else power may be abused. Therefore self-knowledge was among the greatest Aristotelian requisites for good character.

And who is more powerful than a pastor? The pastor stands as priest, as mediator between people and God. The pastor serves the body and blood of Christ at the Lord's Table, holds the keys that bind and loose sin, and is steward of the mysteries of God. We must not let those who are ignorant of themselves be in the morally demanding role of pastor.

Chrysostom once pleaded that he was not a fit subject for ordination because he lacked the requisite discipline and character:

> A priest ought to be sober minded, and penetrating in discernment, and possessed of innumerable eyes in every direction, as one who lives not for himself alone but for so great a multitude. But that I am sluggish and slack, and scarcely able to bring about my own salvation, even you yourself would admit, who out of love to me art especially eager to conceal my faults. Talk not to me in this connexion of fasting, and watching, or sleeping on the ground, and other hard discipline of the body: for you know how defective I am in these matters: and even

if they had been carefully practised by me they could not with my present sluggishness have been of any service to me with a view to this post of authority. Such things might be of great service to a man who was shut up in a cell, and caring only for his own concerns: but when a man is divided among so great a multitude, and enters separately into the private cares of those who are under his direction, what appreciable help can be given to their improvement unless he possesses a robust and exceedingly vigorous character?[9]

Character is essential. We wish it were not so. If only we could devise some scale of measurement, some list of desirable attributes, some clergy code of conduct.[10] Such efforts are mainly interesting as a sign that the moral quality of a profession is already bankrupt. In modernity, through the efforts of people like Kant, it was hoped that we could devise some means whereby we could get good, wise, courageous judgments and actions from people regardless of their history, background, training, character, or self-knowledge. No. There is no procedural, principled means of bypassing the need for character. Procedures and principles are interesting mainly as indications of the sort of persons we hope to be, of the goods that we hold in common and are attempting to affirm in our actions.

Recently a friend of mine, a doctor and former dean of a medical school, was in the hospital for surgery. He checked himself out of the hospital a couple of days before he was to be released saying, "They could kill you in there. There's nobody in there with any sense." I found this amusing since he had a hand in creating the present medical system.

My friend continued, "The night after surgery, this nurse kept appearing and waking me up, every thirty minutes. I asked her not to keep waking me.

"She said, 'I am required to come in every thirty minutes to see if you have had a post-operative stroke.'

" 'Well, what if I had?' my friend asked.

" 'I would have noted it on your chart,' she replied.

" 'And what good would that have done me? Look, people have strokes because their blood pressure is elevated and your waking me up all night is elevating my blood pressure. Get out!' "

One sees this sort of nonsense throughout our society. We so hoped there might be some way to devise a set of rules, an agreed-upon set of procedures, that might enable us to bypass the need for good people. We thought that just by following the right set of rules, anyone could do good.[11]

Perhaps that approach is possible for some straightforward undertaking like auto mechanics (I doubt even that) but the Christian ministry is utterly dependent upon people with the requisite character to be pastors. True, when I take my car in for servicing, if I were forced to choose, I would choose competence over character in a mechanic. I expect that, to paraphrase Luther, most laity would rather have an interesting sermon delivered by a smart rascal than a lousy sermon delivered by a dumb Christian.

Chrysostom rightly sees that competence among clergy is a moral matter. One of the main reasons he offered in evidence for his refusal of the episcopacy was his own lack of ability:

> Now no one would venture to undertake the building of a house were he not an architect, nor will any one attempt the cure of sick bodies who is not a skilled physician; but even though many urge him, will beg off, and will not be ashamed to own his ignorance; and shall he who is going to have the care of so many souls entrusted to him, not examine himself beforehand?[12]

Chrysostom uses Paul as an example of an intelligent, well-schooled person who used a wide range of competence in service to the gospel:

When, therefore, both before working miracles, and after, St. Paul appears to have made much use of argument, how can any one dare to pronounce him unskillful whose sermons and disputations were so exceedingly admired by all who heard them? Why did the Lycaonians imagine that he was Hermes? The opinion that he and Barnabas were gods indeed, arose out of the sight of their miracles; but the notion that he was Hermes did not arise from this, but was a consequence of his speech. In what else did this blessed saint excel the rest of the apostles? and how comes it that up and down the world he is so much on every one's tongue? How comes it that not merely among ourselves, but also among Jews and Greeks, he is the wonder of wonders? Is it not from the power of his epistles? whereby not only to the faithful of to-day, but from his time to this, yea and up to the end, even the appearing of Christ, he has been and will be profitable, and will continue to be so as long as the human race shall last. For as a wall built of adamant, so his writings fortify all the Churches of the known world, and he as a most noble champion stands in the midst, bringing into captivity every thought to the obedience of Christ, casting down imaginations, and every high thing which exalts itself against the knowledge of God, and all this he does by those epistles which he has left to us full of wonders and of Divine wisdom. For his writings are not only useful to us, for the overthrow of false doctrine and the confirmation of the true, but they help not a little towards living a good life. Such are the medicines and such their efficacy left us by this so-called unskillful man, and they know them and their power best who constantly use them. From all this it is evident that St. Paul had given himself to the study of which we have been speaking with great diligence and zeal.[13]

I have therefore told seminarians that their first duty to their vocation is to study, to work hard, to master the material, to be competent. There is absurdity in a seminarian having the liberty to say, "I just don't care for church history courses, so I'm not taking any." Can one imagine a medical student saying, "I don't care for the study of anatomy so I studied microbiology instead"? The medical faculty has enough respect for the demands of medical practice to demand courses in anatomy. Competence is a moral matter.

In his forty-eight chapters on preaching in his *Summa de arte praedicatoria*, Alan of the Isles reserves his strongest words of condemnation for preachers who do not study:

> O vile ignorance! O abominable stupidity! It imposes silence on a prelate, it renders mute the watchdog, the shepherd; it is a frog which, when placed in the dog's mouth, takes away his power to bark. The prelates of our time occupy the chair of the master before they have known the student's bench; they receive the title of teacher before they have worn the gown of the pupil; they would rather stand over than stand with; they prefer the riches of unearned honors to the rewards of dedication. One who teaches without doing contradicts Christ.[14]

But, when it comes to pastors, smart or dumb, there is a link between character and competence that makes character and competence complementary. A person who desires to please God in ministry will desire to acquire those skills that make one an effective instrument for God. On the other hand, the skills required of ministry (like biblical interpretation, homiletical ability, pastoral care) reinforce our love of God and form us into more godly people. As someone who spends much of his time attempting to make future pastors competent, giving them the skills and techniques they need to preach well, I must never lose sight of the peculiarity of what it means for pastors to be competent.

When we examine the skills that pastors need, we can see that even those skills have a requisite character component. For instance, in order to interpret the Bible, pastors are taught certain critical techniques and exegetical methods for getting at the meaning of the text. Presumably anyone, even a scoundrel, could, by using these skills, discover what the Bible is attempting to say.

Not necessarily. An honest awareness of one's prejudices, an admission of one's limitations, a sense of humor, humility, dependence upon the Holy Spirit, and perseverance are all traits of character more than techniques. And all of these traits may be essential to faithful reading of Scripture. I know that one ought not to attempt to read the Gospel of John without a sense of humor.

Athanasius stressed a well-formed character as essential for good biblical interpretation:

> For the searching and right understanding of the Scriptures there is a need of a good life and a pure soul, and for Christian virtue to guide the mind to grasp, so far as human nature can, the truth concerning God the Word. One cannot possibly understand the teaching of the saints unless one has a pure mind and is trying to imitate their life. . . . Anyone who wishes to understand the mind of the sacred writers must first cleanse his own life, and approach the saints by copying their deeds.[15]

Augustine advised that, while we are looking into "the heart of the scriptures" we would do well also to look "with an eye to your own hearts."[16] In other words, who one is (character) makes a big difference in how one is able to understand Scripture. I have been critical of Phillips Brooks's often-quoted definition of preaching ("truth communicated through personality") as lacking much theological substance, as playing too easily into the hands of an American experientialism that always elevates personality over truth. However, Brooks's definition works because it is true that those skills required in order to preach are heavily dependent upon who is doing the preaching. As John Henry Newman put it, "Nothing that is anonymous will preach."[17] The congregation is quite right in expecting that we are at least attempting, to a greater or lesser degree, to embody the faith that we proclaim. The Christian gospel is inherently performative, meant to be embodied, enacted in the world. To speak the gospel skillfully without attempting to perform the gospel is a false proclamation of the gospel.

Lacking a sense of the peculiar shape of ministerial character, bereft of a well-formed church, we become the victims of whatever cultural images of success happen to be in ascendancy at the moment. Hauerwas complains that the main clerical skills today seem to be,

> knowing how to get along with people, rather than constant study of Scripture, liturgical leadership, and discernment of challenges currently facing his or her congregation. Given the undefined nature of the ministerial task today, only a person of character will be able to sustain the discipline necessary for the development of such skills, for ministers are often rewarded more for being personally accommodating than for preaching in an exegetically responsible way.[18]

Certainly, ministers need to be schooled for what they do. Yet the nature of the ministry requires a schooling unknown in some other vocations because of the requisite character required to do the job faithfully. That is why pastors testify that the best schooling they receive tends to be apprenticeship—looking over the shoulders of a master, someone who has mastered the craft of biblical interpretation, or homiletics, or pastoral care, or church history, and perhaps even more so, the art of self-mastery. The word "seminary" means literally "seed bed," a place where masters cultivate new seedlings for future growth and development.

Aristotle taught that character was contagious. We become persons of character by submitting to formation by persons of character, both the living and the dead.[19] When ministerial education degenerates into the mere acquisition of skills—the inculcation of knowledge, data, and ideas—it is detrimental to the formation of pastors. All ministerial education worthy of the name consists of various forms of apprenticeship because the goal is the formation of consistent clerical character.

Ministers, like all Christians, are called to embody the faith that we profess. I remember a book on pastoral care called *The Pastor As Person* that had as one of its major theses that most pastors get into trouble when they forget that a pastor is not only a pastor, but also a *person*. A person of God, yes, but still a person with all of the same needs, desires, and human limits of any person. We pastors must not lose sight of our personhood. Such was the argument.

Yet pastors are interesting because they are persons on whom hands have been laid, a burden has been bestowed. Once we are ordained, our ordination makes us infinitely more interesting persons than we would have been if we had not been so designated. I think most of the ethical problems of pastors are not due to our forgetting that we are "persons," but rather when we forget that we are pastors. We are Christians who are called to the particular service of embodying this faith before the congregation, in word and sacrament. Though pastors may chafe at the burden, there is no way to escape the truth that we are called to be "examples to the flock," as most of the rites of ordination put it, quoting 1 Peter 5:3. The Pastorals repeatedly stress the congruity between right teaching and right behavior by the elders and deacons (or widows). Pastors are enjoined to practice what they teach and preach.

How often, when some pastor commits some public

sin, there is always someone there to trivialize the lapse by saying, "Well, pastors are only human." Not only is this a curious abuse of the word "human," but also a degradation of the ministerial vocation. Pastors are called to be more than "human," as are all the baptized. The waters of baptism, the imposition of hands upon the head, and the gift of the Holy Spirit, make us even more than human, or perhaps more accurately, truly human.

There are those who worry about our supposedly higher standards for clergy than laity. After David Bartlett discusses the rigor of the Pastorals' view of the ministry, as found in places like 1 and 2 Peter, and 1 and 2 Timothy, he says,

> one must ask about the definition of ordination that presupposes a kind of two-tiered Christianity: the relatively moral lay people and the astonishingly moral clergy. Especially for those for whom the gospel consists centrally in the proclamation of God's choice to justify the ungodly, it becomes odd to define that by the heroic godliness of the preacher.[20]

In my church, the day has long passed when divorce was an impediment to a pastoral appointment. A number of our bishops have been divorced and remarried, despite Jesus' clear condemnation of such practice. Yet it is also clear in my denomination's argument over gay and lesbian ordination that, while many of our laity are quite willing to support the full inclusion of gay and lesbian persons in the life of the church, they draw the line at ordination. Is it right to insist on higher, different standards of behavior for those who are the professional "religious," as the Catholic church has traditionally called us, than for the laity?

To be fair to the Pastorals, they appear to be addressed to a community that must rigorously monitor the behavior of its leaders because that community is engaged in a life-and-death struggle with the surrounding, threatening culture. While there is some evidence of accommodation- ism within the Pastorals, they are intensely concerned with the coherence and integrity of the Christian commu- nity. Any revolutionary organization, attempting to sub- vert or to counteract the dominant culture, must be demanding of its leaders because it is demanding of its members. Compromise and accommodation are not val- ued words in such an abrasive gathering.

I suspect that, if the Pastorals were judging our views of clergy leadership, our concerns that the clergy are being expected to be "astonishingly moral people," they would say to us that this is merely evidence of our own accommodated, compromised, and adulterated form of the church. If we have no basic quarrel with the world, then why worry if clergy demonstrate the same sexual promiscuity, serial monogamy, materialism, and greed so vividly on display in the world? No wonder we value being "nonjudgmental" and "gracious" toward sin within the church. Our church morality has become var- ious forms of accommodation to the dominant political and economic order.

When President Clinton's pastor pleaded for us all to show a bit more "love" to our promiscuous Chief Executive, one heard more than a pastor who had allowed himself to be co-opted into an unfortunate posi- tion by a manipulative parishioner, and the pastor's rev- eling in the momentary media spotlight. One also witnessed the emptying of the Christian notion of "love" of any cruciform substance, of any concern for those who had been betrayed by the President's perversion of "love," a perversion made more egregious by the President's frequent invocation of the Christian faith in order to defend his presidential position.

We are not being naively idealistic or demandingly unrealistic when we ask our leaders to be exemplary persons and, when they show that they are not, to ask them to remove themselves from positions of leadership. The needs of the community are superior to the needs of its leaders. Furthermore, the church has the good sense to see that, in placing a person in the position of ministerial leadership, that person is exposed to a unique array of temptations. Chrysostom says that no one would risk an expensive sailing ship by placing it in the hands of a weak, inexperienced, unseasoned captain. For this reason he who is ill-equipped to stand up to the multiple temptations of ministry ought not to be put in charge of a church:

> I know my own soul, how feeble and puny it is: I know the magnitude of this ministry, and the great difficulty of the work; for more stormy billows vex the soul of the priest than the gales which disturb the sea.
>
> And first of all is that most terrible rock of vainglory, more dangerous than that of the Sirens, of which the fable-mongers tell such marvellous tales: for many were able to sail past that and escape unscathed; but this is to me so dangerous that even now, when no necessity of any kind impels me into that abyss, I am unable to keep clear of the snare: but if any one were to commit this charge to me, it would be all the same as if he tied my hands behind my back, and delivered me to the wild beasts dwelling on that rock to rend me in pieces day by day. Do you ask what those wild beasts are? They are wrath, despondency, envy, strife, slanders, accusations, falsehood, hypocrisy, intrigues, anger against those who have done no harm, pleasure at the indecorous acts of fellow ministers, sorrow at their prosperity, love of praise, desire of honor (which indeed most of all drives the human soul headlong to perdition), doctrines devised to please, servile flatteries, ignoble fawning, contempt of the poor, paying court to the rich, senseless and mischievous honors, favors attended with danger both to those who offer and those who accept them, sordid fear suited only to the basest of slaves, the abolition of plain speaking, a great affectation of humility, but banishment of

truth, the suppression of convictions and reproofs, or rather the excessive use of them against the poor, while against those who are invested with power no one dare open his lips.[21]

I agree with Chrysostom's exceedingly high view of the moral requirements for clergy, not because clergy are fated to be some upper crust of morally exemplary Christians, but rather because their vocation, as leaders of a countercultural community, demands certain morally strenuous attributes. The needs of the church are for those who are well-formed in the Christian virtues, are honest enough about themselves to lead the congregation in confession, and who, having received enough of the grace of Christ to be gracious with the sins of others, are courageous enough to speak the truth in love, while remaining attached so securely to the Word that they love the truth of Christ even more than their congregation's affections. Rigorous moral demands go with the territory.

Chrysostom notes that an athlete who never competes in public will never be tested and therefore will never be proved as an athlete. But when that same athlete strips naked to compete in a contest, then the whole world sees his strengths and weaknesses. It's an earthy image by which Chrysostom points to the peculiarly public quality of the Christian ministry whereby, when a pastor ascends the pulpit to preach, the pastor's moral flaws become more pronounced, more visible for all to see:

> For it is quite impossible for the defects of priests to be concealed, but even trifling ones speedily become manifest. So an athlete, as long as he remains at home, and contends with no one, can dissemble his weakness even if it be very great, but when he strips for the contest he is easily detected. And thus for some who live this private and inactive life, their isolation serves as a veil to hide their defects; but when they have been brought into pub-

lic they are compelled to divest themselves of this mantle of seclusion, and to lay bare their souls to all through their visible movements.[22]

When Paul makes the rather arrogant sounding demand of his flock to "imitate me," in places like 1 Thessalonians 1:6, he does so, not simply out of apostolic arrogance (though I would be the last to say that Paul is free of such a failing), but rather out of the peculiar nature of gospel ethics. He says in Philippians 3:17, "become fellow imitators both of and with me and observe those who walk according to the pattern *(typos)* you have in us" (my translation). What they are to imitate is Paul's attempt to conform his life to the cross of Christ. He makes this sort of bold cruciform argument in Philippians 2:1-13 where Paul urges, "Let the same mind be in you that was in Christ Jesus." The one who "emptied himself" and "took the form of a slave" is the one whom we are to imitate in walking a narrow, cruciform path that few in the world wish to walk. Embodiment, imitation, inculcation are unavoidable for all the baptized, especially the baptized who are called to lead the baptized.

Few have been more scathing than Søren Kierkegaard in denouncing and satirizing clergy who thought that ordination somehow excluded them from the demands of exemplary crossbearing. "It is absolutely unethical when one is so busy communicating that he forgets to be what he teaches " (p. 350), said Kierkegaard.[23] He seems suspicious of people who "talk the talk, but do not walk the walk" as it is sometimes said in the African American church. He continues,

> Christianity cannot be proclaimed by talking—but by acting. Nothing is more dangerous than to have a bunch of high-flying feelings and exalted resolutions go off in the direction of merely eloquent speaking. The whole

> thing then becomes an intoxication, and the deception is
> that it becomes a glowing mood and that they say, "He is
> so sincere!" (p. 350)

Kierkegaard even charges that the reason why we preachers love to preach before large congregations is that if we were forced to say what we preach in an empty room we would "become anxious and afraid" upon being forced to listen to what we preach. We would be horrified to learn that the gospel is meant to be applied to ourselves. Then he warns, "It is a risk to preach, for as I stand up.... I have one listener more than can be seen, an invisible listener, God,... This listener pays close attention to whether what I am saying is true, whether it is true in me.... He looks to see whether my life expresses what I am saying.... Truly it is a risk to preach!" (p. 354).

Aristotle believed that it was too much to expect ordinary people (that is, most of us) to be good. About the best one could expect of ordinary people are good habits.[24]

When my grandmother was told that someone was ill or in declining health, she would say, "I fear they have been neglecting their habits."

Some of us clergy have been neglecting our habits, ethically speaking. Financial malfeasance, sexual impropriety, and simple neglect of pastoral responsibility plague our profession. Henry Lyons embarrassed his entire denomination by being convicted of various forms of thievery, while blaming his crimes upon the media and racism. At the beginning of my ministry, a much admired bishop who was head of the National Council of Churches was forced to resign due to marital infidelity. A 1990 poll in our church reported that 42 percent of the clergywomen surveyed said that they had been harassed by other clergy and 17 percent of female laity reported being harassed by their clergy. Yet in my experience these spectacular moral lapses are not the main ethical problem among the clergy. Our infidelities are more mundane, less noteworthy but no less detrimental to the body of Christ. They are primarily due, not to dramatic propensity to sin but mostly to a weakness of character, the failure to persevere, to keep at the challenges of ministry when things are difficult. A number of laity have been deeply damaged by the sexual improprieties of their pastors. But one can scarcely conceive of the millions of laity who have been exposed to the moral ravages of bad sermons, sloppy administration, and careless pastoral care.

When a candidate for ministry who appears to have an eating disorder comes before the Board of Ministry, ought we inquire into that person's physical well-being? Certainly, Paul urged us to "glorify God in your body" (1 Cor. 6:20*b*). He was talking about marriage at the time, but is not abuse of the body a serious matter? Does the person's condition speak of a disorder that spells trouble for the future of this person's ministry? That ought to be the main question in most discussions of ministerial morality. Is a person's character an aid or a hindrance to service to the congregation?

This is one of the things that troubles me in my own church's current discussions of homosexuality and ordination. I find little biblical basis for singling out homosexuality as a special sin that precludes ordination. One would be on much more firm biblical ground, according to the Pastorals, to exclude from leadership those who are greedy or who have committed adultery. First Timothy would surely regard with disfavor those candidates for ministry who were so poorly prepared in seminary, or so intellectually indifferent as to be unable to teach sound doctrine.

Discernment of the characters of those who are called to the ordained ministry ought to be left to the ecclesial

51

bodies that are charged with examining candidates for ministry, not to enforcement of lists of rules. A person of homosexual orientation who was living a life of sexual abstinence could make a remarkably good candidate for ministry. Living as we do in a society that elevates a person's sexual orientation as the supreme mark of humanity, it is countercultural, radical, and downright faithful to encounter a person, more disciplined than myself, who is willing to forgo worship of Eros in order to serve the church.

## TRAITS OF CHARACTER

John Wesley spoke often of "the marks of a Methodist," those traits of character that ought to be stamped indelibly upon the baptized. Ethics, being a matter not just of what we do but also of who we are, leads us to ask, What sort of people ought we preachers be in order to faithfully lead our church into the next century? What character traits are peculiar to those who lead in the name of Christ?

In the chapters that follow, I will utilize Richard B. Hays's framework for New Testament ethics, the three focal biblical images of *community, cross,* and *new creation.* Let these images serve as the peculiarly Christian lens through which we look at the ethical challenges of ministry. Community, cross, and new creation will give content to our discussion of ministerial character, serving as the specifically Christian theological claims that both form and require specifically Christian traits of character.[25]

1. **The church is called to be a countercultural community.** Jesus came to reconstitute Israel, God's covenant people. Concrete embodiment, enfleshment, is required for a people who are called to present to the world a visible alternative to the world's arrangements,

52

and that embodiment is not just within individuals, but within a corporate body.

"Present your bodies as a living sacrifice, holy and acceptable to God.... And do not be conformed to this world, but be transformed by the renewing of your minds," is the way Paul puts it in Romans 12:1-2. He speaks, as the New Testament usually does, in the plural. As Hays says, when it comes to specifically *Christian* ethics the question is never initially, "What should *I* do," but rather "What should *we* do?"[26] Most of a pastor's time is spent worrying about community, trying to keep the church together, attempting to build consensus, struggling to include new life in the congregation, shepherding the flock. The pastor is uniquely the "community person"[27] by virtue of ordination, the one who is charged with cultivating those communal virtues that make the church the church.

This ecclesial stress upon community is inherently countercultural in a world of self-made men and women, rugged individualism, and cultured narcissism. Pastors are those who tend to think, not for ourselves, but with the church, seeking communal discernment, cultivating a dependence upon the wisdom of the saints in all that we do. The church—body of Christ, People of God, Sheep of the Fold, and Bride of Christ—tends to be more important than either I or my occupational advancement.

2. **Jesus' death on the cross is the paradigm for faithfulness to God.** Paul refers to the "community of his sufferings" (Phil. 3:10 AT). That's the church. We are to be those who embody Jesus' self-giving love, giving even unto death. We are to take up the cross daily and follow. Sacrifice is not a thing to be avoided, as it tends to be in our culture, but rather the means by which God has chosen to save the world. Fidelity is not a matter of efficiency, results, or success, but rather a matter of congruence with the way Jesus lived and died.

Hays quotes Paul's "While we live, we are always being given up to death for Jesus' sake, so that the life of Jesus may be made visible in our mortal flesh" (2 Cor. 4:11), calling this "the vocation and job description for the church."[28] The cross keeps judging our lapses into a theology of glory, keeps setting before us the narrow way of a suffering God, keeps mocking our clerical lapses whereby we substitute worldly wisdom for gospel foolishness. The cross unmasks the evil behind worldly standards of success and achievement. In the light of the cross, economics becomes a spiritual issue. My salary is a spiritual matter on the basis of a cruciform faith. The kind of car that I drive is a matter of ministerial morality.

3. **Though we have not yet been fully redeemed, the church already embodies the power of Jesus' resurrection.** Though we are in suspense in the time between Jesus' resurrection and his *parousia,* we can affirm with Paul that anyone in Christ is already participating in new creation. We already have the "first fruits of the Spirit," though we still "groan inwardly while we wait for adoption, the redemption of our bodies" (Rom. 8:22-23). Although we continue to be impressed by the "not yet" quality of the promised new age, we also know something that the world does not, namely, that, in raising Jesus from the dead, the powers that be have been doomed, defeated by God; something is afoot. The church is that peculiar place where, in its rites, rituals, and life together, "the ends of the ages have come" (1 Cor. 10:11).

As new creation, the church keeps being prodded by resurrection faith to be discontent with present arrangements, to keep standing on tiptoes looking for final and consummate redemption. At the same time, in our failures, in our suffering and trials, we are not permitted despair. The same God who raised Jesus from the dead, thus vindicating his peculiar way of life and death, will also, we believe, raise us. So on Sundays we lift up the cup of bloodred wine and "proclaim the Lord's death until he comes." Pastors, as all Christians, work in that hope-filled interval between Christ's resurrection and the world's complete new creation.

Ministry is difficult. Therefore the great challenge of ministry is to be the sort of characters who can sustain the practices and virtues of ministry for a lifetime. What we require is some means of keeping at ministry— preparing and delivering sermons, visiting the sick, counseling the troubled, teaching the ignorant, rebuking the proud—even when we don't feel like it, even when it does not personally please us to do so. Fortunately for the church, Easter will not let us give up, though we have ample reason, in the present age, to do so. We are not permitted to give up on ministry because God, if the story of Easter is as true as we believe it to be, doesn't give up on ministry in the world. As prisoners of hope, we keep working in the expectancy that God's kingdom will come, that God's will is going to be done on earth as in heaven. In us, in our feeble ministrations, God is getting back what belongs to God.

In the rest of this book we will move through these three focal points for New Testament ethics, attempting to draw out some of the implications for who pastors are and how we ought to act, moving from the peculiarly Christian affirmations of faith, to those habits and virtues that adhere to these affirmations. Specific clerical ethical dilemmas will be discussed as instances and exemplifications of the ways that our peculiar commitments to Christ cause us to lead the church in ways that are congruent with our commitments.

Because I agree with the late Iris Murdoch when she said that most of the really interesting moral work goes on before we arrive on the scene of an ethical decision, my stress will be upon the character of those who are doing the deciding and the acting rather than upon the procedures that ought to be employed when pastors are in an ethical quandary. I believe that pastors are more interesting than the ethical dilemmas in which they find themselves. Because I also believe in the witness of the saints, the powerful ethical import of those who have walked before us in this demanding, glorious vocation, at the end of each chapter, I will turn toward one of our calling whose work encourages us. This brings me to Bessie Parker.

## BESSIE PARKER: A CLERICAL CHARACTER

In a most gracious way, God has this way of taking the stuff of our character that we present at ordination, and using this, remaking and remolding that, using us for divine purpose. According to one of my ministerial mentors, Carlyle Marney, "God will use any handle to get hold of somebody." Divine persistence and resourcefulness are, according to Scripture, virtually without limits. Bessie Parker was the handle that God used to take hold of South Carolina for more than thirty years of ministry until her death a decade ago.

Bessie, who entered the pastoral ministry in 1956, went through automobiles the way her Methodist circuit riding ancestors went through horses, routinely driving forty thousand miles every year, taking the gospel to places named Twitty, Brown Swamp, Indian Field, and Aynor—the kinds of places that the U.S. Postal Service has difficulty locating, but the Lord does not. Although she had a reputation for being one of the most effective preachers in the South Carolina Conference, she was the bane of bishops. Churches fought the bishop when they heard they were getting a "lady preacher," but the fights were always worse when, four years later, the bishop dared to move "our dear, Reverend Parker" somewhere else.

With snow-white hair and soothing, Southern voice, Bessie was everyone's stereotype of what a grandmother is supposed to be, a fact used for everything it was worth. Preachers stood in line to enlist Bessie to lead their annual mission funds appeal. When she got to preaching, telling you how much you were going to enjoy sending breeder pigs down to Haiti ("They will go down there and make more piggies in the name of the Lord," Bessie giggled.), pigs started packing. Her counseling skills were legendary.

Bessie specialized in engineering marital reconciliation. "Always take a homemade pie with you when you counsel people with serious problems," she advised younger ministers. When the people of one church repeatedly refused to fix their leaking roof, members were scandalized by the sight of their pastor, white hair, blue jeans, and all, atop the church roof on a Monday morning hammering away. The roof was quickly repaired with the willing assistance of everyone. "It just don't look right to have your grandmother up fixing your roof," one church officer commented.

Toward the end of her ministry, the bishop sent Bessie to a very difficult church, one that had a reputation for feuding, contentiousness, racism, and animosity toward the denomination. Before Bessie arrived, they had literally run off two preachers in six months. They had consistently refused to send any money to support the programs of the denomination. To me, it seemed a cruel thing for the bishop to send Bessie there just before her retirement. Everyone predicted disaster.

A few months passed without a word from Bessie. Then, I saw her at a church meeting and, fearing the worst, asked her how she was getting along at her new appointment.

"The sweetest people I have ever seen!" she said. "Our first work team will leave for Brazil next month. I've got to get back there early because this is our music weekend with the neighboring Black congregation."

I was dumbfounded. Could she be talking about the same church? What about their hatefulness? Their racism? Had there been *no* problems?

"Not really," replied Bessie. "There was one little misunderstanding when we voted on this year's budget."

"Misunderstanding?"

"Yes. We got to the apportionment for the Black College Fund. When we were asked to vote on acceptance, the chairman of our board said, 'Reverend Parker, we don't give no money because we ain't paying for no niggers to go to college.'"

"Oh no! And what did you do?" I asked.

"I stood up and said, 'John, that's not nice. You sit down and act like a Christian.' Everything else passed without a single problem."

Who's going to misbehave in front of their grandmother?[29]

Richard Baxter advised his seventeenth-century reformed pastors that, "the tenderest love of a mother should not surpass ours," for our people. Bessie routinely mothered her people toward the kingdom, using any handle she could get to get across the gospel—just like God used Bessie. That she was a woman, a mother and grandmother, a widow, all these human attributes were caught up by the grace of God into her vocation. What is more, her church at last (it only took 1,956 years!) recognized those attributes as having potential for the pastoral ministry. She was willing to have her life caught up in the purposes of God for the world. Hers was a character formed by God for good.

The Scriptures are a complex, polyphonic presentation of Jesus and his way, a presentation too complex to be encapsulated in any interpretive synthesis—even in community, cross, and new creation. However, Christian discipleship involves the creative synthesis, in our churches and in our lives, of the diversity within the canon. What we call "ethics" is the imaginative construction of a person in community. We must be humble in such an undertaking, for it is of the nature of Christian ethics that we so easily get things all wrong, so desperately require the communal admonition and correction that is the church in its life together. What we call "ethics" is a mode of embodied prayer. In ethics, as in prayer, we are in continual conversation with the saints, the "quick and the dead," the tradition, and the living Christ as we keep living out the question, How then shall we live?

The goal of such deliberation is not that we apply community, cross, and new creation in such a skillful and inclusive way that we have left nothing out of our ethics, that we have no doubt as to the basis for our characters. The goal is performance, embodiment, to be as we profess, to walk as we talk, that we come to imitate the worthy example of a Bessie Parker.

Simply by telling you the story of Bessie, I have performed an ethically significant act. By listening to this story, you are becoming a more interesting and more faithful person than you would have been had not you heard the story. Bessie's witness is becoming part of you. You will act differently because to some degree you are different. Stories of the saints have their way with us. Characters like Bessie help to render us characters who know the cost of discipleship and are willing to pay the price.

The content of clerical character, the formation of those who embody Christian community, cross, and new creation in their lives, is the concern to which we now turn.

# CHAPTER THREE

# The Pastor in Community

Jesus is depicted in the gospels as assembling a new community, reconstituting a scattered Israel, recalling those who had been excluded, and inviting everyone to the table. Christian ethics is inherently ecclesial, communal. Israel knew there could be no Messiah without the constitution of a messianic community. God's peculiar means of saving the world is through a family, a people reconstituted by Jesus. This manner of salvation is fundamentally Jewish. The way that the world is to be reclaimed is through the formation of a holy people, a kingdom of priests that shall be a light to all nations. This prophetic language of election is enlisted by Christian communicators in places like 1 Peter 2 and applied to the church. In Scripture, God's way of being universal, for all people, is through a particular people, Israel and the church.[1]

If Mark is the Gospel of the cross, then Matthew and Luke come to mind as Gospels of the new community in Christ. Great authority is given to the community in matters of ethics, but that authority rests upon the astounding promise that, "where two or three are gathered in my name, I am there among them" (Matt. 18:20).

Great demands are placed upon the community because Jesus is with us until the very end of the age (Matt. 28:20). Church is the way Christians do politics, the way we present a living, breathing, political alternative to the powers that be.[2]

Christians have no way of knowing what is "good" before we know the church. We are forbidden to hold some *a priori* notion of "justice," or "peace," or "righteousness," then to ask how the church might be helpful in enabling us to attain that notion. Rather, it is the church's witness to Jesus that gives content to such high-sounding words. It teaches us to define words like "justice" as "thy kingdom come," "righteousness" not as "the greatest good for the greatest number" or "equal pay for equal work," but rather as "thy will be done on earth as it is in heaven." We do not desire to come to that modern place where we allegedly "think for ourselves"; rather we want to think with the saints, to think faithfully with the church, to submit all of our images of righteousness, success, and good to the scrutiny of the church's story of salvation in Jesus.[3]

One sees the communitarian basis of Christian ethics most explicitly in Paul. For Paul, most ethics is intra-church ethics. Time and again his test for the ethical appropriateness of a given practice is, Does this edify the body? The foundational Pauline metaphor for the church is "body": "Now you are the body of Christ and individually members of it" (1 Cor. 12:27). He even evaluates worship practices like the Lord's Supper and speaking in tongues on the basis of how well worship builds up the body.

In the letter in which Paul evokes most strongly the image of the church as body, Paul writes twice, "'All things are lawful,' but not all things are beneficial" (see 1 Cor. 6:12; 10:23*a*). He adds to the second instance, "'All things are lawful,' but not all things build up" (1 Cor.

10:23*b*). In the first instance, Paul is concerned with the ethics of the body and the perils of bodily self-indulgence. In the second, Paul addresses the pastoral problem of whether or not it is right to eat food offered to idols. Paul agrees with his Corinthian opponents that Christian freedom is a great virtue. Yet his stress upon the "body," the church, trumps even so noble a virtue as freedom. Too often the freedom of the strong can be detrimental to the weak in the community. The conscience of the weak, in Paul's advice to the Corinthians, restrains even gospel-given freedom. As Walter Brueggemann puts it in his discussion of these passages, "the reality of the community comes before any liberty, and certainly before the liberty of any autonomous individual."[4] This is rather amazing when one considers Paul's high regard for the peculiar freedom of a Christian.

Obviously, there is no room in this communitarian ethic for modern, Western concepts of the freedom of the autonomous self, or for the liberal attempt to distinguish between "private" and "personal" ethics on the one hand and social or public commitments on the other. It is difficult to imagine a truly isolated individual who is unattached to some communal, social framework. Even the person who says, "My behavior is my own business and no one else's," is thereby demonstrating his attachment to a "community," namely, the community that fosters isolated, unexamined, lonely people whose only purpose is self-aggrandizement. In a capitalistic, subjectivistic culture, the church's goal is to make all ethics "public," that is, communal, a function of what ought to be happening in the church. Ordination makes pastors intensely public figures. It is not fair for us to complain on the one hand about the "fishbowl" that is life within the congregation in which everyone seems to be peering into the pastor's private world, while on the other hand attempting to serve as an example to the flock.

The communal mentality that is the church raises questions about our defense of pastoral confidentiality. In a society of strangers, one ought to take care in telling secrets to strangers because knowing a secret gives one power over another. Do not tell secrets to those who may use those secrets against you. Thus, attorneys tend to see client confidentiality as a major aspect of the American judicial system.

Yet the church is more of a family than a conglomeration of strangers. A family tends not to have secrets among those in the family. A great deal of pastoral care has as its intent to help personal pain go public. No pastor functions as a lone agent in the pastor's care of those in need in the congregation. Sometimes there are others in the congregation whose ministry is more effective than the pastor's in some area of human need. In my last congregation, when someone had a problem with alcohol, I usually attempted to put that person in touch with someone else in the congregation who had experience and expertise greater than mine with that affliction. If a person insists on complete secrecy in a pastoral counseling session, I feel it my duty to warn that, (1) secrecy is difficult in a well-functioning congregation; and (2) secrecy tends to cut off the person in pain from the congregational resources for healing.

All sorts of conflicts between one good and another are connected with issues of secrecy, lying, and confidentiality. The movie, *Priest,* is a powerful depiction of the dilemma of a pastor who is confronted with conflicting claims related to the abuse of a child in his congregation. While I would never unilaterally reveal some secret told to me by a parishioner, I believe that often it is my task to urge persons in pain not to suffer their pain in loneliness. Suppression, denial, and sublimation tend to be enemies of health and healing and all of them rely upon the conspiracy of silence and secrecy. Time and again, Paul uses the metaphor of the body to teach the church that many of our actions are ethically significant, from a Christian point of view, only as they relate to the needs and cares of others. It may be of no consequence to my soul that I eat meat offered to idols (to take one Pauline example), but it is of great consequence that my "freedom" is a cause of harm to others in the body. The same could be said of secrets. The norm that is applied in issues of secrecy is not only the "rights" of the individual but also the building up of the body, including the incorporation of those who feel alienated from the body. Too often secrecy serves to protect the stronger members of the congregation instead of the weaker.[5]

I believe that confidentiality is more an issue of prudence than secrecy or rights. Prudence involves knowledge of the parties involved, self-knowledge, and honest assessment of the right means to a good end. Aristotle notes that, in acting ethically, it is of great importance to know people, in their specificity and peculiarity. General rules, generally applied, are no substitute for wise discernment within each ethical dilemma. Through our pastoral work, we have the opportunity to be with our people in a wide array of circumstances that give us a wonderful standpoint from which to give them moral guidance. It helps to know who people are, where they have come from, and whom they hope to become in order to judge what is "right" in each case. The pastor has a unique vantage point from which to observe people. Jesus said that the good shepherd is able to say, "I know my own and my own know me" (John 10:14). Thus, the pastor's communitarian duties provide a superb position from which to be a moral guide and resource for the congregation. One of Aristotle's analogies for good ethics was learning to ride a horse. One cannot learn to ride a horse apart from submission to a master in the art, apart from getting to know the unique qualities of the animal, the feel of the reins in the hand, the strengths and weaknesses of horse and rider together. This is a dynamic, deep mode of moral discernment that seems peculiarly appropriate to the practice of the parish ministry.

It helps to be attached to some larger vision of what the church ought, by God's grace and our fidelity, to be. The church is called to pioneer forms of community and human relationship that are impossible in most worldly arrangements. We strive to be a community of truth, where the truth can be told in love, in order that the body might be built up into Christ. Note the way that Ephesians links truth telling with maturity as the Pauline metaphor of the body is developed in relationship to truthfulness:

> But speaking the truth in love, we must grow up in every way into him who is the head, into Christ, from whom the whole body, joined and knit together by every ligament with which it is equipped, as each part is working properly, promotes the body's growth in building itself up in love. (Eph. 4:15-16)

These passages judge our willingness to endure immature, poorly developed Christians rather than to love the body of Christ enough to tell the truth. While it is no easy matter to keep truth and love together, my impression is that most of us opt for a sentimentality we call "love" rather than telling the truth. The therapeutic is more important than the truthful. Ephesians reminds us that dishonest love is a major impediment to Christian growth.

## A COMMUNITY OF PREACHERS, A COMMUNITY OF HEARERS

The Reformers defined the church as that place where the word is rightly preached and the sacraments duly administered. Right preaching requires the existence of a community of truth. It is a great challenge to be called by God to be a truth teller in a world of lies. We clergy could not tell the truth were it not for a God whose gifts enable us to be truthful.

December, Second Sunday of Advent, a prickly text from Malachi, jerks me by my clerical collar, shakes me up and down, and speaks:

> But who can endure the day of his coming, and who can stand when he appears?
> For he is like a refiner's fire and like fullers' soap;...and he will purify the descendants of Levi and refine them like gold and silver, until they present offerings to the LORD in righteousness. Then the offering of Judah and Jerusalem will be pleasing to the LORD as in the days of old and as in former years. (Mal. 3:2-3)

Don't worry, I assured my December congregation, the prophet is not talking about you. A wrath-filled God is coming to the temple, but not for you. God is after those who make their living at the temple, *the clergy.* "He will purify the descendants of Levi and refine them...until they present offerings to the LORD in righteousness" (3:3). We priests, contemporary "descendants of Levi," who live off religion, praying, prophesying, preaching, making offering to God in behalf of the people squirm when Malachi raves about the "priests, who despise my name. You say, 'How have we despised your name?'...By thinking that the LORD's table may be despised....I have no pleasure in you, says the LORD....I will not accept an offering from your hands" (1:6-7, 10). God says to us clergy, in essence, "You wear me out" (1:13).

"The lips of a priest should guard knowledge, and people should seek instruction from his mouth, for he is the messenger of the LORD of hosts. But you have turned aside from the way; you have caused many to stumble by your instruction" (2:7-8), says Malachi. (Here, of course, the prophet is speaking of clergy who are also professors of theology in seminaries.)

After the prophet takes a swipe at priests who have committed adultery and fooled around with various members of the choir (2:14-16; you can look it up), then begins the Advent call from Malachi. "Who can endure the day of [the LORD's] coming? . . . He is like a refiner's fire, . . . like . . . soap . . . and he will purify the descendants of Levi." (3:2-3).

Shortly after the night I was ordained, pharmacists bested clergy in the annual list of the "most admired" professions. Then we were beaten in the "most admired" list by firemen, letter carriers, and Amway distributors.

At the beginning of each year, *The Christian Century* has a recap of the most significant religious news from the past year. In the top religious stories of a couple of years ago, one story concerned a number of prominent priests who were charged with sexual abuse of children. Other stories told about a major embezzlement case at a large church in the Midwest; malfeasance at the National Council of Churches; and clergy-laity trysts in Texas. We mainline clergy snickered when the news was of the sexual shenanigans of TV evangelists, but this story was close to home—involving mainline liberals—and none of us laughed.

When a fellow United Methodist preacher from Fort Worth bit the dust last fall after his multiple sexual harassment episodes were made public by some courageous women, his fall hardly merited the headlines, so many of his fellow clergy had fallen before him.

A friend of mine, an economist, was asked to serve on the board of a church charitable organization that helps needy children. His first days on the board were a sort of religious conversion experience for him, so inspired was he by the work of the organization, so impressed was he by the tremendous amount of need. But then he learned of the salaries, the real salaries of some of the clergy staff. He uncovered accounting irregularities. After prayerful consideration, he brought it to the attention of the directors and was dismissed from the board.[6]

He told me, "I think clergy, because they tell themselves that they are doing the work of the Lord, are particularly susceptible to self-deceit. If you're feeding hungry children, none of the moral rules apply to you which apply to other mere mortals."

On a Sunday not long ago, I preached on forgiveness. The text was Jesus' counsel to forgive seventy times seven times (Matt. 18:21-35). As people filed out after the service, a woman came up to me and asked, in a voice that seemed to me to contain more than a touch of aggression, "Do you mean to tell me that God expects me to forgive my abusive husband who made my life hell for ten years until I got the guts to leave him?"

I immediately moved into a defensive stance, mumbling something about, "Well, that's a tough issue all right. And I can't possibly say everything that ought to be said on such a big subject. But I do feel, or at least it sounds to me like Jesus is saying, with his talk of so much forgiveness, that . . . I mean, he does tell us to forgive our enemies and I can't think of a much greater enemy for you than your ex-husband."

"Good," she said, "just checking!" and she proceeded confidently out the door.

That woman reminded me of my high vocation. It is not my task to protect her from the rigorous demands of discipleship, by paternalistically saying to her, "Oh, that's right. You are an abused woman. I'm sure Jesus did not intend for you to bear moral obligation. Your abuse makes you a victim, not a moral agent."

She refused to be let off the hook so easily. She refused to let me relieve her of her baptismal vocation, rejecting my rather blasphemous temptation to imply that Jesus did not know what he was doing when he called her to be a disciple.

Malachi, and the words of a Yahweh worn out by clergy and their self-justification, summons us preachers to examine the curious connection between the practice of homiletics and clerical ethics. Malachi calls us back (or is it *forward?*) to clerical lives grasped by something greater than ourselves or even our condescending desire to protect our people, namely our vocation to speak and to enact the Word of God among God's people. We would be better people, you and I, if we were more faithful preachers.

Homiletical habits—disciplined, weekly study; honesty and humility about what the text says and does not say; confidence in the ability of God to make our puny congregations worthy to hear God's Word; a weekly willingness to allow the Word to devastate the preacher before it lays a hand on the congregation—are habits, skills of the homiletical craft that form us preachers into better people than we would be if we had been left to our own devices. This is the sort of thing Paul was getting at when he told the Corinthians that it would have been nice if he could have preached to them with flattering, eloquent words but, being a preacher he single-mindedly "decided to know nothing among you except Jesus Christ, and him crucified" (1 Cor. 2:2).

We live in a culture of deceit. In such a time, it is easy to lose our way. Therefore we preachers would do well to cling to our vocation, to determine to know nothing save that which the church has called us to preach, to serve the Word before we bow before other gods.

Who could blame the great God for being worn out with us clergy (Mal. 1:13)? Our poor preaching, Malachi indicates, is not just a matter of lousy homiletical technique, it is also a failure of character, a moral matter of tragic proportions. Yet this scathing prophetic rebuke by Malachi of false prophesy is also combined with hopeful prophetic promise. The Lord may even yet purify us descendants of Levi, may soap us down, fire us up, call us back to our chief task—to be yoked so securely and joyously to the Word that in the process of proclamation of the Word, we become the Word as it dwells in us richly.

A primary means of the Word dwelling among us richly is the witness, rebuke, correction, and encouragement of the saints—saints departed like Malachi, saints still among us like a contemporary disciple who will not let me relieve her of the burden of her baptism. Their words enable us to speak the Word. Truth telling is a community matter.

## CLERGY COLLEGIALITY

As Christ's new community, we are bound to one another, as the foot is bound to the eye, as the eye is bound to the heart. In my own denomination, the Wesleyan connection, we place great stress in our ecclesiology (if not always in practice) and upon collegiality in our ministry. As members of a Conference, we are supposed to be mutually accountable in covenant with one another. I am called to submit my personal goals and ambition, my individual needs, sometimes even the needs of my family, to the needs and goals of the Conference. The good of the church is more significant than my own. John Wesley established a tradition of collegial accountability for us clergy. Today, a singular mark of any "profession" is that profession's ability internally to credential, examine, and police the members of the profession. My work is judged by standards higher than those of my own devising. Self-examination is rarely as effective as communal examination.

Perhaps this is a prejudiced and somewhat gratuitous Methodist observation, but I wonder if the moral lapses one often observes among clergy of those free-standing, independent congregations, whose pastoral leaders have no link with other pastors, are due to the historical anomaly of detached, unaccountable clergy. At crucial moments congregations must be protected from demagogic clergy by other clergy. Any ecclesiastical system that has no structural means of clergy supervision of clergy seems an odd and ethically dangerous arrangement.

Yet even in my native connectional church system, all is not well. One aspect of our current crisis of ministry, in many Conferences today, is that the laity have lost faith in our ability to supervise and to hold accountable our colleagues. In my church I have seen clergy who are guilty of gross moral impropriety be forgiven, excused, and exonerated by their fellow clergy with little regard for how such moral laxity will effect the congregations who are the victims of these immoral leaders.

We say that we excuse because of "love," or "grace," but the usual reason we do so is that we have an ecclesiastical system that is dominated by the self-interest of the clergy, where it is more to our clerical advantage to blink at the immorality of our colleagues than to discipline them. We show amazing grace toward clerical malfeasance and little concern for their congregations.

I once thought that our inability to discipline our own was due to mushy Methodist ideas of "grace." In the church, discipline and law are means of grace, not its antithesis. But I have now come to believe that the cause of this inability is even more serious. We have so little respect for our own calling, so little sense of awe for the sanctity of our ordination, that we are unable to muster much righteous indignation for those who violate our vocation. What we ought to say is not, "Jesus forgives you and therefore we forgive you—after you have had a year of church-sponsored counseling." We ought to say, "We have so much respect for our vocation that to allow you to continue in it would demean the sacrifices we have made to be ministers—to say nothing of the sacrifice of Jesus."

In deliberations regarding clergy immorality within my church, and there are no deliberations except for the most heinous of sexual immorality or financial impropriety, the inevitably cited text is John 8:7, "Let anyone among you who is without sin be the first to throw a stone at her." This then leads to a sentimental universalization of this episode in order to silence any debate on the morality in question.[7]

The verse in competition with this one is, of course, "Do not judge, so that you may not be judged" (Matt. 7:1), an equally effective terminator of ethical deliberation. Citation of these passages, universalized, sentimentalized, and taken out of context, perverts them into an overall dominical command not to make ethical distinctions. The result is that these verses trump any other ethical concerns. Matthew 7:1 is a warning that those who judge, which includes us all, shall stand under the judgments of God. A chill ought to go down the spine of a church that demonstrates its spinelessness in dealing with clergy immorality.

If we are quoting Scripture on such occasions, we ought to be quoting Matthew 18:15-17:

> "If another member of the church sins against you, go and point out the fault when the two of you are alone. If the member listens to you, you have regained that one. But if you are not listened to, take one or two others along with you, so that every word may be confirmed by the evidence of two or three witnesses. If the member refuses to listen to them, tell it to the church; and if the offender refuses to listen even to the church, let such a one be to you as a Gentile and a tax collector."

Community is a great virtue, but in order for there to be community, there must be limits upon the community. A community with no boundaries for appropriate community behavior is no community. Note that Matthew 18 is the only place in all of Scripture that we find Jesus using the word "church." Paul cites this procedure when pleading with the Corinthians (1 Cor. 6:1-8) to settle their disputes like Christians rather than to involve the pagan judicial system. We also find reference in James 5:19-20.

What may sound, in Matthew 18, like harsh exclusion is in reality a church that relentlessly attempts to keep community Christian. Here, there is no attempt to keep things quiet, to smooth over true conflict, to deny the wrong. There is a premium here on direct confrontation. If confrontation with the offending party fails, then others are brought into the discussion. The issue thus quickly becomes public, a matter of group, communal concern; not a private matter to be fought out by individuals. The wronged party does not have to summon up the courage to set things right. At the second stage the community takes upon itself the burden of the conflict. Note that with each step, the circle of people involved in the dispute grows. What began as a private matter becomes a congregational issue. When one member of the congregation is in pain, the whole church is in pain.

There are conflicts when it is not clear—as is implied in Matthew 18—just who is wrong in the dispute. Thus Matthew 18 presents conflict resolution as a process, a rather involved and detailed process over time, with an ever-widening circle of conversation. Matthew 18 also reminds us that all efforts at reconciliation and restoration do not work. We are the people of God but we are not God. We cannot create reconciliation, cannot demand it. In such cases, we are not merely treating people as "a Gentile and a tax collector," we are not giving up on them.

We are giving them up to God, giving them and the injustice over to a God who is more resourceful and inventive in working reconciliation than we can ever hope to be.

In my experience, the sort of persistent efforts to confront and to reconcile, to restore the break in community, are rare in the church. More often, there is denial, a conspiracy of silence. We are willing to tolerate a fractured community rather than risk a test of our Christian ability to be agents of reconciliation.

When clergy are accused of ethical wrongdoing, there ought to be a fair, truthful investigation of the facts. Certainly, some moral lapses are not of as great an import as others. Circumstances, intentions, church law, consequences, in short, all of those criteria used to judge the behavior of any Christian ought to be applied. However, the church ought not to shrink from using criteria based upon the peculiar high calling of pastors, criteria related to the communal purpose of pastors, in order to specially judge pastors and to hold us accountable.

If, after all of this, a member of the clergy has been judged to be guilty of a severe moral lapse, that person ought to be removed from the ministry. We do so in grief, that someone having once been called to the high task of pastoral leadership has forsaken that calling. Yet we also act on the basis of two cardinal ethical presuppositions in regard to clergy. To put the matter bluntly: The welfare of individual pastors is not as important as the good of the church as a whole. This sounds strange in a culture where the individual is the supreme concern of society. In the church, matters are different. Pastors exist for the sake of the community of faith and, when their behavior is injurious to their effectiveness as leaders of that community, their ministry as leaders has ended. When we judge our sisters and brothers in the ministry in this way, it is our contention that not to judge them would be a denigration of their vocation as Christians.

Pastors who sin may be forgiven of their sin, in the manner that any Christian may be forgiven. Their forgiveness can serve as a witness to other Christians of the power of God to forgive even the worst of sin and to grant new life in Christ. But they probably cannot continue to serve as clergy. Having forfeited the honor and the trust of leadership, they must find other ways to exercise their Christian discipleship.

In my own church, I have seen bishops and Annual Conferences fail to censure even gross ministerial immorality, pleading for "compassion" toward the offending clergyperson. Alas, "compassion," in our hands, too easily slips into vague sentimentality and ethical "know-nothingism." Furthermore, their compassion is misplaced. They find it expedient to be compassionate to their fellow clergyperson because there is a reciprocal arrangement within the clergy guild—I will tolerate your misbehavior if you promise not to raise questions about mine. Our compassion would be more theologically defensible if it were not for the struggling Christians who are attempting to live the faith amid great difficulty and who deserve the best in pastoral leadership.

A Board of Ministry struggled with how to place a pastor who was blind. It was not that the man was blind, it was that, unlike many sight-impaired persons, his blindness was used by him to be totally dependent. Living alone, at his first church, he depended upon the members of the church for most of his necessities. Members drove him to all of his pastoral engagements, performed all of his errands, did all of his shopping, then subsequently labeled each item in Braille when it was placed on the shelves of his parsonage.

After two years, the church pleaded with the clerical administrators for a different pastor. They argued that the entire purpose and mission of the church had become subsumed into the care and sustenance of their vision-impaired pastor.

Some on the Board of Ministry argued that such service ought to be considered a privilege by a church. Others argued that the issue was mainly one of "justice" for the pastor. Some argued that the church ought not to allow such conditions as blindness even to be discussed. Eventually, a nonparochial position was found for him, funded for the most part by the church at large. Unfortunately, there was little confrontation with the man's irresponsibility. Thousands of poorly sighted persons function quite well in a variety of demanding positions by acquiring the skills and support required.

The main questions ought not to be about the professional aspirations and needs of the pastor, but rather about the missional needs of the church. In my own biblical interpretation, I find that I most often err in performing an individualistic reading of biblical texts that were clearly intended as an address to the whole church, rather than to isolated individuals. I am conditioned by my culture to ask, "What does this mean for me?" rather than to ask the corporate, "What is the Bible saying to us?"

In like manner, most of our ethics are far too individualistic. Our concerns, as pastors, ought to be primarily corporate and communal before they are to be individual. I recall the church leader who, under the banner of clergy collegiality, urged his pastors, "never to criticize or speak ill of a fellow clergyman, never to receive members from his church if they should try to leave his congregation and come to yours, always to do all you can to help a colleague succeed in his ministry."

While I may agree with most of his sentiments, I have learned that collegiality means much more than tolerating clerical incompetence and providing a united clerical front against the laity and their criticisms of my fellow pastors. Our concern for our colleagues in ministry is not only for them as individuals since, as individuals, as we have said, we are not that important. Our concern is for the community, the gathered body of Christ, that it may flourish, that it may accomplish its God-given mission, and that it may have the leadership it deserves. Collegiality means accountability to my ministerial peers, a willingness to expose my ministry to their critique and guidance. It also means responsibility for critique and guidance of my fellow pastors.

Sexual misbehavior among the clergy is a serious matter, not because we have some higher expectation for the sanctity of clergy, though such expectation is appropriate. Rather, sexual immorality among clergy tends to be an offense against the community, a fundamental reproach to the communitarian vocation of pastors. Because pastors are placed in positions of power over people, including many people in great need, it is more onerous when they use such positions to prey upon others for their own sexual gratification, and the community is correct in taking grave offense.[8] Pastors who can only sometimes be counted upon to keep their marriage vows, who are only sometimes safe to be left alone with vulnerable people, ought not to be pastors. Any community or association of clergy that allows such persons to remain in positions of pastoral leadership demeans the vocation of the whole body of Christ.[9]

Here is Rebekah Miles's succinct, good advice for pastors concerning sexual misconduct in ministry:

### PRACTICAL STEPS FOR PREVENTION, ACCOUNTABILITY, AND JUSTICE

Establishing the ground rules:

- It is never appropriate to have sexual contact with parishioners.

- It is always the pastor's responsibility to keep the appropriate boundaries.
- Pastors and other leaders are also responsible for setting up and following procedures to hold pastors accountable.
- No pastor or church is free from the risks of misconduct. The only responsible path is to be aware of the problem, vigilant about prevention, and tenacious in following procedures of accountability.

## WATCHING FOR PROBLEMS AND WARNING SIGNS

A crucial step is simply to be self-aware. Know the risk factors and warning signs.

Watch for signs that you are attracted to a parishioner. Do you take more care with your appearance when you expect to see this parishioner? Do you anticipate being with this person? Do you find excuses to be around her or him? Are you secretive about the level of interest and interaction? Would you be uncomfortable if others knew about the intensity of the relationship? If you are aware of enduring attraction, move immediately to establish better boundaries. Work to establish more appropriate avenues for intimacy in your own life.

Watch for signs that parishioners might be attracted to you. The same questions that you asked of yourself also apply to the parishioner. If the person seems to be unduly attracted, be extremely clear about boundaries. Read about the dynamics of transference and countertransference so you can recognize them.

Be especially vigilant in times of personal vulnerability. If you are lonely, depressed, or in crisis, be all the more attentive to the preventative steps and warning signs. Find an appropriate place to talk about problems and temptations.

Be particularly attentive if the parishioner is having marital problems, is in crisis, or seems particularly vulnerable.

Whatever the attraction, it is always the pastor's responsibility to keep the boundaries.

## FOLLOWING STEPS FOR PREVENTION: THE INDIVIDUAL CLERGYPERSON

Establish procedures of accountability for yourself. Make rules about interactions with others. Watch for warning signs. Find responsible ways to be intimate with others.

Be self-aware when forming close friendships with parishioners. Find people who are healthy and mature. Dual relationships between pastor and parishioner carry risks. Know the risks and respond accordingly.

Find a trustworthy confessor to talk with when you are attracted to someone or when facing other problems. Make sure the confessor shares your moral assumptions about faithfulness and sexual boundaries and will also hold you accountable.

If you counsel parishioners, have regular supervision with a licensed supervisor. Ask the church to pay for it.

Set up your office and counseling procedures to protect yourself from misconduct or the appearance of misconduct. Counsel in your office only when other people are in the building. Leave your door unlocked. Consider getting rid of blinds or curtains.

If you need to meet a parishioner outside the office, find a public place. If a parishioner comes to your home, make sure someone else (a spouse or trusted church member) is in the next room, the blinds are open, and the doors are unlocked.

If you need to visit individuals at their homes and have reason to be uncomfortable, take another parishioner with you.

If a situation feels wrong or strange, trust your gut instincts and keep very strict boundaries. If appropriate, refer to another counselor or giver of care.

If you are uncomfortable or sense that the other person is uncomfortable, refrain from touch. In private settings, be particularly cautious. Whatever the setting, follow the other person's lead on whether to shake hands or hug. When hugging, use a side hug, or one in which the shoulders touch, instead of frontal hugs where the chests touch.

Be cautious about some discussions of sex. Of course, in Sunday school discussions or counseling it is sometimes appropriate, but be thoughtful.

Whatever your sexual orientation and gender, take precautions with men and women. Just because you are not attracted to those of the gender you are counseling, does not mean they are not attracted to you. Also, the purpose of these steps is not only to avoid misconduct but also the appearance of misconduct.

Know and follow the procedures of your denomination or church.

Take care of yourself. Find Sabbath time. Pray. Cultivate ways to relax and relieve stress. Find responsible channels for intimacy.[10]

Ironically, the communitarian basis of Christian ethics is often appealed to as the reason why clergy immorality ought to be ignored—it will harm the church as a whole to reveal this pastor's sin. This is a tragic distortion of the ethics that ought to characterize life in the body of Christ. Alasdair MacIntyre, a communitarian and virtue ethicist par excellence, stresses that two types of precepts arise from the church's stress upon community. Those of us in the church need two sets of ethical precepts:

> [1.] On the one hand they would need to value...
> those qualities of mind and character which would con-

> tribute to the realization of their common good or goods. That is, they would need to recognize a certain set of qualities as virtues and the corresponding set of defects as vices.... [2.] They would also need however to identify certain types of action as the doing or the production of harm of such an order that they destroy the bonds of community in such a way as to render the doing or the achieving of good impossible in some respect....
>
> The response to such offences would have to be that of taking the person who committed them to have thereby excluded himself or herself from the community.[11]

There can be no real Christian community without the possibility of exclusion, painful though that may be. It is an interesting commentary on our system of values that, despite my diatribe against our laxity in regard to sexual sin, in my church family that is about the only sin that clergy can commit that leads to loss of ministerial credentials.

The corporate, communal basis of Christian ethics not only requires us to deal severely though justly with those who violate the bonds of Christian community, but also encourages us to judge ourselves, to inquire into our responsibility for lapses in clergy morality. We in the church not only have a responsibility not to deny or excuse clergy misconduct. We also have an obligation to ensure that we develop those supportive networks and the training needed to help clergy develop the skills and insights needed to conduct ourselves in a manner that always upbuilds the church. Studies indicate, for instance, that where denominations have openly addressed issues of clergy sexual misconduct and offered training to address the issue, such training had remarkably positive effects.[12]

Plagiarism by preachers is a serious matter, not primarily because thereby a preacher has stolen material that is owned by another, but rather because such use of material without attribution is a violation of the community of preachers. The acknowledgment of my indebtedness to the work of a fellow Christian is my way of affirming, before the congregation, the communion of saints, my demonstration of my dependence upon the community of preachers, living and dead, for my homiletical thoughts. While we may have debates over precisely what usage ought to be given attribution, and how to give attribution in a sermon without laboriously and unnecessarily burdening the sermon with overzealous annotation, there ought to be no disagreement that I need to look for ways to show the congregation that my thoughts are not my own, that I think with the saints, that I submit to the wisdom of the past as well as the body of Christ as a whole every time I attempt to bring the gospel to speech.

Criticism of the church is, for me, an even more difficult issue. As leaders of the church, we bear the responsibility to help the church be self-critical, be all that the church is called to be. Yet when does one cross the line, in one's criticism of the church, from having a lover's quarrel with the bride of Christ to being disloyal, spiteful, and divisive? I do not know. Perhaps I am merely demonstrating my own failings when I say that, in my church, I do not see a great peril from a too critical clergy, but rather from clergy who are far too easily pleased, who seem to have little disagreement with present arrangements, and who think that it is their job as ecclesiastical leaders to suppress all criticism, debate, and reform.

In debates about the present shortcomings of the church and its future, we need to fight like Christians. We ought not to demonize our opponents. We ought to be fair and thoughtful in our criticism, taking pains not to bear false witness. We ought to love those with whom we disagree enough to express our disagreements with them openly, rather than passive-aggressively as so often is the case with clergy arguments. We ought to constantly examine ourselves in such debates, realizing how easily self-interest clouds our judgments, asking ourselves if our positions are taken out of a genuine attempt to be faithful to the will of God and to see the best for Christ's body, the church.

Clergy are probably the least supervised, the least collegially connected of any of the professions. Those who practice medicine learn quite early that one of the cardinal principles of medicine is openness, a constant willingness to have a colleague look over one's shoulder, to have one's work evaluated by one's physician peers. We clergy could profit from a new awareness of the communal character of our work.

This makes all the more tragic that pastors are some of the loneliest people in the church. An ethic of character demands the practices of friendship. Nearly one-fifth of Aristotle's *Nicomachean Ethics* (books VIII-IX) concerns friendship. The demands of ministerial character are so great that they cannot be met without daily, sustained interaction with those whose values are our own and in whose company we flourish.

So much of a pastor's work involves feeding others, reaching out to their needs, giving of self, teaching, and sharing one's time and energy in service to the church. Therefore the pastor needs friends. Friendship tends to be intrinsically valuable; it is engaged in for its own delight. In friendship, the pastor, who has so often been giving to others, receives, and is nourished by others.

Aristotle, while noting the intrinsic, non-instrumental quality of friendship, also underscored the usefulness of friends in making us more virtuous people than we would have been without friends. Friends listen to us when no one else will, they give and seek advice, and they tell us things no one else cares enough about us to dare to tell us. In all these activities, virtue is being developed as a sort of gracious by-product of friendship. Because we enjoy what our friends enjoy, virtuous friends cultivate in us new virtues. Friends are a sort of moral mirror, showing us our virtues (and vices) in ways that no one else can. Friends expose their lives to our gaze as well.[13] We know our friends all the way down— their secrets and their inner lives. They thus provide us an imaginative example of what it is like to live lives different from the ones we were given before we met our friends. Because we love our friends, we want to be the best we can be for them, and thereby our friends encourage the best in us.

Because of the particular demands of a pastor's role, it is sometimes difficult to make true friends of one's parishioners. Because of the clerical competition that sometimes infects those of us within the same denomination, it may be difficult to find clergy friends within one's own church family. However, find friends we must. The ordained ministry is too morally demanding to be practiced in isolation, alone and without the essential interaction, critique, and support that friends provide.

The pastor who claims to be either too busy to cultivate friends, or too immersed in the duties of the ministry, is likely to be the pastor who is avoiding the truthfulness and the prodding that are natural components of friendships. Christians, tied as we are to life in the body, are prejudiced toward the conviction that there can be no moral life worthy of the name that is individual. Christian ethics is communal ethics. Wise ethical discernment and courageous living are gracious derivatives of the practices of friendship.

## OUR LIVES ARE NOT OUR OWN

How can clergy possibly persevere amid the great demands of the church? Paradoxically, one of our major moral resources is the church—the church that has ordained us, called us forth to leadership, keeps calling us, keeps authorizing us, keeps empowering us to be better than we would have been if we had been left to our own devices.[14] In expecting us to be truthful, courageous preachers, the church makes us truthful and courageous. In the church's weekly routine of worship, forcing us to worship a real God every seven days whether we feel like it or not, the church keeps some of us close to the wellsprings of the faith even when we have been negligent to avail ourselves of those restorative waters. In demanding that we stand between them and God, our people make us priests, and we are thereby surprised by our own priestly effectiveness, despite ourselves.

Being effective "despite ourselves" is one of the great gifts of being a pastor. Not long ago, when someone was busy taking me apart at the front door of the church after a sermon, I thought to myself, "That's rather amazing. I, who seem to be constitutionally conditioned to want to please everyone, have actually angered someone because I said what was maddening but true. This church has actually made good old, compromised, flatterer me into one who can sometimes be a speaker of truth."

The Enlightenment invented the notion of the unfettered "Man Come of Age"—humanity without some external authority to which obedience is owed, particularly without reference to the external authority of the church. Descartes, Locke, and Kant all contributed to this elevation of the free and unattached subject who is subject to nothing and lord of all. Freud gave such philosophy popular expression with his theory that human maturation requires increasing emancipation from extrinsic communal authority. All communal, social restraints upon the personality are forms of external repression.

85

Postmodernity has noted that such unfettered freedom is an illusion. There is no person without context and commitment. Modernity's liberation only resulted in a host of cruel conformities, few of which acknowledge themselves as conformity. The self is largely a social construction, so the issue is never, Will I be conformed to some external determination? But rather, To which social conformity will I be attached? In this sense, all ethics is "communal," that is externally, socially imposed.

One of the unfortunate consequences of Augustine's assertion of an indelible character bestowed upon the clergy in ordination, an assertion that I praised in the previous chapter, is that, as the church moved through the Middle Ages, it tended to make ordination a personal possession of the individual apart from the community by which and for which it was conferred. Clergy were seen as some sort of upper crust of the laity, a detached class that functioned with its own internal standards of ethics.

Here we have attempted to stress the importance of the church as the source and the purpose of clergy. The ordained ministry is a function of the general ministry of all the baptized. Clergy activity is "good" or "bad" on the basis of what needs to happen in the church, not on the basis of some detached clergy code of conduct that is severed from the needs and vocation of the gathered congregation.

Sometimes the Christian ethic of nonviolence, indifference to riches, or truth telling is ridiculed as being impractical, idealistic, or hopelessly heroic. Christian ethics is inherently ecclesial rather than heroic. It is precisely as lone, detached individuals that we are the most immoral. A clerical ethics is not intended to make sense apart from a church that makes it make sense. Stanley Hauerwas convinced me that Christian ethics is utterly "unintelligible divorced from such a community."[15] We ought to placard over all Christian ethics, "DON'T TRY THIS AT HOME." That is, do not try to live nonviolently, simply, or graciously without a community strong enough to back you up in such endeavors. Do not try to be extraordinarily faithful apart from a community that is extraordinarily forgiving. Violence, servility to the powers, and deceit come quite naturally to us. The lone individual, attempting to stand alone, is no match for the subtle and persistent pressures of the empire. Do not attempt to protect the life of the unborn apart from a community that assumes responsibility for those who are ill equipped to have children in isolation and loneliness. It is the church that makes Christian ethics make sense.

Martin Luther King Jr. intended to lead the quiet, scholarly life of a professor, perhaps one day to be president of Morehouse College. Yet providence placed him, for the time being, in a rather forlorn little church in Montgomery, Alabama. Shortly after he arrived, a woman was put off a city bus in accordance with the city's racial separation laws. She was a local activist, Rosa Parks. A meeting was held in one of the city's African American congregations. Angry, frustrating words filled the air. What were they to do? Someone thought that it would be nice to have the new young preacher in town say a word before they went home. Martin Luther King, newcomer that he was, was reluctant to speak, but he agreed. Someone present that night said that shortly after King began to speak, this disheartened, confused crowd began to be a movement, a movement that would, in just a few years, shake the world. Martin Luther King that night was "ordained" to lead and thereby became a leader.

If it were not for the authorization, the evocation, the forgiveness, the grace, and the faith of the church, clergy ethics would seem a ridiculous expectation. The good news is that even for ethically ordinary people like most of us pastors, the production of saints is possible.

For me, this moral formation occurs most vividly in the corporate worship of the church. While I am, on most Sundays, so busy leading the congregation in worship that I sometimes have scant opportunity to worship, worship I do. In bending my time all week to the study and exposition of the Scriptures in preparation for preaching, in my leadership in corporate prayer, in my service at the Table, in my work at the baptismal font, I am being formed. It takes time to worship, at least an hour on Sundays; a lifetime of weekly bending of one's life toward God, of following a way that is against our natural inclination. In taking time for such practices, we literally retake time, sanctify time as God's.

In this rhythm of work and worship, Sunday praise and Monday performance, as well as Sabbath rest, Christian character is being formed. So the late John Howard Yoder called our worship, "the communal cultivation of an alternative construction of society and of history."[16] In Duke Chapel where I try to preach, the glorious stained glass windows contain images of saints like Moses, Deborah, Miriam, and Joshua. This means that, while I preach, these saints look over my shoulder, urging me on, to be sure, but also judging me, setting my life alongside the canon of their witness. I would be nothing as a preacher, without the help of the saints.

When I studied ethics in seminary, I got the erroneous impression that ethical deliberation was mostly a matter of pairing down one's possible courses of action to the single best action. Ethics occurs during those frustrating times of life when one is presented with a couple of possible alternatives and is forced to choose between them.

But what if some of our best ethical work occurs, not as we narrow our possible options, but rather when we expand our possibilities? What if ethics is more a matter of effusive imagination than careful elimination? When I say, "This was the only thing I could do, considering the circumstances," what I am saying is, "I am a person of limited experience and imagination, therefore this appeared to be the only thing I could do."

Sunday morning worship, with its rich array of metaphors, symbols, stories, images, and ideas tends to seed and to stoke the imagination, to fund our store of ethical alternatives. Once again, I am helped in my preaching by the building in which I preach. I can't get in on Sunday morning without pushing past statues of Savonarolla, Wycliff, Wesley, and Luther. The smell of burning clerical flesh is unmistakable at the entrance to our chapel. For me, this is good.

A young man once said to crusty old Tertullian, "I would be Christian, but there are limits. A man has to live, doesn't he?"

"Do you?" replied Tertullian.

Some of us are perishing in our ministry, not because we lack commitment or courage, but simply for want of imagination. We just can't conceive of lives other than the ones we are living.

When the young Gandhi appeared before a judge in South Africa in the early part of the twentieth century, the judge heard his case and said that though he regretted to send Gandhi to jail for his protest against racial apartheid, "I have no other alternative."

Respectfully, Gandhi said, "Well, you could resign your office."

## AGAINST THE CHURCH IN ORDER TO BE FOR THE CHURCH

While Scripture is both the product of and the authorization for the church, it also manages to be the church's most severe and truthful critic. Judgment tends to begin with God's own house. Clergy are often placed in the peculiar ethical role of having to support and to love the church by castigating and condemning the church.

I heard a bishop tell his pastors, "If you just love your people, everything else will work out in your ministry."

We wish. For one thing, what does the bishop mean by "love"? Jesus was busy loving Israel when he turned over the tables of the moneychangers in the Temple. Where do we find the resources, in our service to the church, to serve the church by withstanding the church?

Clergy must have character strong enough to help form the character of the congregation. A compromised clergy produces a compromised church. Bad character is contagious. There was a time when I thought the image of the pastor as empathetic "enabler" was a good image for ministry—the democratic enabler, standing in the wings, not on stage, humbly prompting the laity in their ministry.

Yet I observed, in my visits to congregations, that strong leaders tend to evoke strong congregations. The pastor must do more than merely "enable." The pastor must model, embody, demonstrate, and thereby evoke the ministry of the laity. Some pastors get the congregations they deserve. And the same could be said for congregations. We pastors are frighteningly dependent upon the discipleship expectations of our congregations.

So a major challenge for pastors is to form congregations whose discipleship gives dignity to the sacrifices we have made in giving our lives to this ministry. Congregations must have the character that makes them worthy to be led by pastors of well-formed Christian character.

It takes quite a congregation to know that the pastoral ministry is not primarily about popularity. The laity must be convinced that the demands of their discipleship are so great that they deserve the very best of pastoral leadership in order to equip them for their baptismally bestowed vocations.

As Hauerwas says,

> questions of ministerial morality are not only about the persons who enter the ministry; they are also about the Church, for the church must be composed of people who require their minister to do the unpopular thing. A ministry of character is only possible if we are a people of character.[17]

What are the clerical habits that ought to be cultivated if we are to be people who have been well formed by the community of faith? I have mentioned our weekly leadership of corporate worship as one habit that keeps putting us pastors in our place, ethically speaking. Our peculiar service is service to the people of God and our particular ethic is derived from that service.

For me, it is pastoral visitation, putting myself at the disposal of my people, that I find most ethically formative in the communal sense. I consider it essential for the task of preaching that I be present in the homes and workplaces of my people. One can learn more about someone in a living room than in years of momentary encounters at the door of the church.

I find it humbling and humiliating to have to place myself and my time at the disposal of my people. I trudge about the neighborhood, knocking on doors, sometimes becoming the victim of their dogs. Some pastors reassure themselves by saying, "Pastoral visitation is a thing of the past. People don't want to see their pastor in their homes."

I fear this is pastoral wishful thinking. In visitation, I send a signal to my people. I tell them, I want to know you, as you are, where you are. I am making myself available to you and to your life. I am exposing myself to you on your own turf. My counseling load increases and my sermons improve after a week of steady visitation.

At the same time, I am also sending a signal to myself.

As I knock on parishioners' doors, wondering if they will open them to me, as I get my nose rubbed in their daily lives, as I intrude into that space some would like to keep private, I am being reminded of the peculiar nature of my vocation. I am not some detached, "professional" keeping office hours. I am a pastor, shepherd of the flock, the one who is charged with helping them to embody the faith into the world, their world. I am not a "professional" who guards my "professional distance" between me and my "clients." I am a pastor in service to the congregation that has been gathered by the Word of God.

For all these reasons, I regard pastoral visitation as an ethical activity.

## "WHO LYNCHED WILLIE EARLE?"

When I was a youth, growing up in Buncombe Street Methodist Church, a pastor visited us to preach for our Youth Week. He was Hawley Lynn. Lynn was introduced as a graduate of Yale Divinity School and a Phi Beta Kappa. Even young as I was, I knew that meant that he was smart. I even remember the subject of his sermon: how we should serve God throughout our lives.

Much later I learned that Hawley Lynn was a servant of the truth. At daybreak on a Monday morning in February 1947, in a place not too distant from the home where I had been born the year before, a group of White men from Greenville, South Carolina, broke into the Pickens County jail, took the jail's lone prisoner, a Black man named Willie Earle, and lynched him on a road between Greenville and Pickens.[18]

In response to the lynching, thirty-one-year-old Hawley Lynn, having recently arrived at the Methodist Church in Pickens, called together a meeting of "public-spirited citizens, both men and women" on February 20.

The meeting was rather quickly adjourned when the mood turned ugly, principally because it evoked defensive sentiments among some of the gathered White citizens who remembered a similar lynching of a Black man in a nearby town some years earlier.

Hawley Lynn felt compelled to speak the Word of the gospel to this horrific situation. Two Sundays later, he preached to his congregation this sermon: "Who Lynched Willie Earle?" In his sermon, Lynn outlined the religious roots of American democracy. He castigated those who refused to shoulder any guilt in the affair by blaming the violence upon "citizens of another county" or "a lawless mob." He noted that "the lynching of Willie Earle didn't begin on February 17" in the context of racial segregation. In a long, winding sermon, Lynn repeatedly asserted that it was the "good," "Christian" folk of his community whose silence, acquiescence, and fear helped to lynch Willie Earle.

It was a rather amazing sermon in the middle of a solid, mostly silent South. Lynn not only preached but also wrote "A Prayer for the Sin of Lynching," which he published in the *South Carolina Methodist Advocate* and in the local newspaper in Pickens.

You may not have heard of Hawley Lynn. Although a version of his sermon was later published in Charles Clayton Morrison's *The Pulpit,* few beyond the bounds of his little congregation benefited from his courage. Yet for a preacher, this is benefit enough, that the flock committed by Christ to our care should be able to hear the truth of Christ. The congregation is not only dependent upon our ministerial fidelity, but sometimes is the source of our fidelity as we pastors are reminded of what a treasure is committed to our care—not only the treasure of the gospel, but also the treasure of the gospel's people, a treasure that is borne, to be sure, in earthen vessels, but a treasure nonetheless.

A key moment in the process of my own ordination occurred on the night I was ordained, as the bishop instructed me, using the words of the ancient ritual, saying, "Never forget that the sheep committed to your care are the ones for whom Christ died."

There I was, wondering if I would be a success at ministry, wondering if the church would adequately appreciate my gifts, wondering where the bishop would send me next. Then the words of the ritual, pounding in my brain, set my puny sacrifice in context. Never forget that the ones who are committed to your care are none other than those for whom he died. It is a gracious, terrifying, wonderful thing to have such trust placed upon the one who is called pastor.

CHAPTER FOUR

# Crossbearing and the Clergy

I was having a difficult time in my previous congregation. A stormy board meeting was followed by a poorly received sermon, which was then succeeded by a none-too-pleasant public confrontation with the chair of the church trustees. What had I done to so badly manage the congregation? I sat in my office, going over the events of the past week, attempting to take appropriate responsibility for the administrative mess I was in. Could I have been more discreet? Why had I felt the need to bring things to a head now? Had I abused the pulpit in last Sunday's sermon?

Then I returned to my preparation for next Sunday's sermon. Year B of the Common Lectionary, Mark. Another story of Jesus' teaching and healing. Another story of rejection. Then it hit me. Why was I so surprised that our congregation was full of conflict? Was the conflict a sign of my failure to skillfully manage congregational differences, or my skillful pastoral telling of the truth? I heard Mark ask, "What's the problem? You think that you are a better preacher than Jesus?"

> "If any want to become my followers, let them deny themselves and take up their cross and follow me. For those who want to save their life will lose it, and those who lose their life for my sake, and for the sake of the gospel, will save it." (Mark 8:34-35)

At that moment I recalled that just about 99 percent of Mark's Gospel encompasses the preparation to crucify Jesus, Jesus' crucifixion, or the aftermath of Jesus' crucifixion. The cross, it appears, is not optional equipment for a faithful ministry. The cross, the self-giving, emptying of God in the crucified Jesus—God's great victory over sin and death through divine suffering—is the primary ethical trajectory of the New Testament.

Paul spends much of his pastoral time attempting to referee in congregational squabbles. In places like 1 Corinthians he pleads for love and unity among the baptized. He tells them that they are all members of one body. He urges them to agree in the Lord.

But it is also clear that one thing Paul values even more than unity, concord, peace, and love is the gospel. Community can be demonic. Not all unified, internally loving "communities" are truthful communities. Even better than community is gospel. "Gospel," for Paul, means cross and resurrection, and perhaps predominately, the cross. For the sake of the cruciform gospel he is willing to provoke division, call names, condemn, accuse, and judge. Paul reminds me as preacher and pastor that I must be tethered to something more significant than peace and harmony if I am to be faithful to my vocation. In the last few years, more than one United Methodist bishop has convinced me that there is a dark side to episcopal calls for unity, concord, and inclusiveness. These words—at least when spoken by many bishops—are code words that mean silence all criticism, drive out dissent, and subordinate the gospel of Christ to niceness.

For Paul, the cross is not only something that God

does to and for the world, unmasking the world's gods, exposing our sin, and forgiving our sin through suffering love, but also it is the pattern for Christian life. He could say, "I have been crucified with Christ; and it is no longer I who live, but it is Christ who lives in me. And the life I now live in the flesh I live by the faith of the Son of God, who loved me and gave himself for me" (Gal. 2:19-20, as translated in the NRSV footnote).

## FOOLS FOR CHRIST

On Good Friday, 1994, Father Carl Kabat, dressed as a clown, hammered on a Minuteman II missile in North Dakota. For his clowning around, Father Kabat got five years in prison.

This sort of pastoral activity is not without precedent. One of the first things Paul says to the Corinthians is that the cross is *moria*, foolishness:

> For the message about the cross is foolishness to those who are perishing, but to us who are being saved it is the power of God. For it is written,
> "I will destroy the wisdom of
>     the wise,
>   and the discernment of the
>   discerning I will thwart."
> Where is the one who is wise? Where is the scribe? Where is the debater of this age? Has not God made foolish the wisdom of the world? For since, in the wisdom of God, the world did not know God through wisdom. God decided, through the foolishness of our proclamation, to save those who believe. For Jews demand signs and Greeks desire wisdom, but we proclaim Christ crucified, a stumbling block to Jews and foolishness to Gentiles, but to those who are the called, both Jews and Greeks, Christ the power of God and the wisdom of God. For God's foolishness is wiser than human wisdom, and God's weakness is stronger than human strength. (1 Cor. 1:18-25)

One night I had a graduate of the university speak to the undergraduates on how she had left a spectacularly successful job on Wall Street in order to return to seminary. She now worked in the mountains of West Virginia among a group of impoverished little congregations.

At the end of her talk, many of the undergraduates expressed anger at her. They told her she was "irresponsible," that she had "wasted a great education." In other words, they got the point. Such a pastor—such a fool—is a living reminder that the gospel is not establishment but revolt, not settled accommodation but rather destabilization of present arrangements.

As Bonhoeffer put it, it is no small thing that God "allowed himself to be pushed out of the world on a cross."[1] Or again, Paul, "God chose what is foolish *(moria)* in the world to shame the wise" (1 Cor. 1:27).

One of the earliest of crucifixes shows Jesus on the cross with the head of an ass. The Letter to the Hebrews says that Christ was crucified "outside the  city gate" (13:12). He was "outside" in more ways than one. He, who entered Jerusalem on an ass, died as an apparent failure.

There was a kind of playful foolishness in him and his teaching of wasted seeds in an act of thoughtless, random sowing. He told of an unproductive fig tree buried in a foot of manure, and for him it was a theological point.

He said that the kingdom of God is like the story of the man who gave a party where nobody came, so the lord of the banquet got mad and invited in all the folk whom you wouldn't be caught dead with on a Saturday night. That's the kingdom of God.

It wasn't that Jesus was being unreasonable, it was that he was exercising a different kind of rationality than that of the world. After one has made a statement like, "God was in Christ, reconciling the world to himself," then all worldly rationalities are thrown into conflict and everything is up for grabs.

Yet there is this relentless tendency for the Christian faith, in our hands, to be transformed from sign of outrage and contradiction, insubordination and usurpation, into (in Tom Wright's words) "the cement of social conformity." The temptation to be "conformed rather than transformed" (*contra* Rom. 12:2) is rather relentless. Church is forever in danger of degenerating into Rotary.

American church historian Brooks Hollifield has chronicled the story of how American clergy have always conformed to the culture, blended into the wallpaper, taking models for themselves from the culture's definitions of success. In the nineteenth century, when business was all the rage, Christian clergy became men in three-piece suits with briefcases, hurrying to catch the next appointment. We became a "profession." In the mid-twentieth century, when the culture fell into the grip of the therapeutic, we became counselors, therapists with clients and good listening skills; anything in order to be someone useful, anything in order not to appear foolish.[2]

Years ago, my professor of pastoral care wondered why so many pastors wanted continuing education in pastoral counseling. He surmised, "Because counseling is the last socially approved activity in which pastors engage."

A certain sort of foolishness is required for Christian ethical thought and action, a playful readiness to roam, to revise, to see odd connections in things that were not seen before, a willingness, a joy even, to be odd. I wonder if one of the ethical challenges for ministry in the mainline church is the sort of people we attract to ministry. We seem to have a high proportion of those who wish to keep house, to conform, and too few who like to play, confront, disrupt, revise, and foolishly envision.

As Paul says, "God chose what is foolish in the world to shame the wise" (1 Cor. 1:27). Elsewhere Paul bragged, "We are fools for the sake of Christ" (1 Cor. 4:10).

I know a pastoral couple who talked their congregation into hiring both of them, each at half salary. They did this in order that both of them might equally share in the tasks of parenting their children. To their surprise, their arrangement turned out to be a witness in their upwardly mobile, career-obsessed congregation. A number of couples in the congregation, upon observing their marriage, decided to enter into similar arrangements themselves. Two pastors, one salary; is this foolishness, or a witness?

Tom Wright suggests that we honor St. Simeon Salos, a Palestinian monk of the sixth century who threw nuts at the candles during the sacred service and ate sausages publicly on Good Friday—all in an attempt to relativize our attempts to take ourselves too seriously. Then there was St. Andrew the Fool who strolled naked through Constantinople and lived as a beggar. Wright says these holy fools kept alive the scandal of the naked, accursed savior who was killed outside the camp. Is it not the death of Christian morality to take ourselves and our acts too seriously?

While at the home of Sir Thomas More, Erasmus penned, *Enconium Moriae,* "In Praise of Folly." Says Erasmus,

> No morons so play the fool as those who are obsessed with the ardor of Christian piety to the point that they distribute their goods, overlook injuries, . . . make no distinction between friends and enemies, . . . . What is this if not insanity? No wonder that the apostles appeared to be drunk with new wine and Paul seemed to Festus to be mad.[3]

From a theology of the cross point of view, what ought to look foolish is a self-satisfied, protected, affluent clergy who have been ordained to take up the cross of

Jesus and follow. Søren Kierkegaard mocked the dissonance between the cross and some of the prominent clergy of his day:

> In the magnificent cathedral the honorable and Right Reverend Geheime-General-Ober-Hof-Pradikant, the elect favorite of the fashionable world, appears before an elect company and preaches with emotion upon the text he himself elected: "God has chosen the base things of this world, and the things that are despised"—and nobody laughs.[4]

I therefore consider it ethically significant that, in my denomination, we clergy publish our salaries. This is what we call collegiality. Unfortunately, we do not do much about the disparity in the salaries of the lowest-paid clergy and the highest-paid, nor do we hold in prayer those clergy (like me) whose relatively high salaries place them in situations of greatest moral peril.

## THE MATTER OF MONEY

To engage in the practice of Christian ministry in a consumptive, materialist society is daily to be reminded of the oddness of the cross. In a world where people are taught that a person's worth consists in the abundance of that person's possessions, the self-giving, self-sacrificial quality of Christian ministry is unavoidably countercultural. Sacrifice and relinquishment come with the territory. However, it is the curious claim of Christians that in such relinquishment, in letting go of those things for which the world so madly grasps, is our true freedom. In the sacrifices of ministry, some of the rewards of this culture are lost, but much good is gained. So Paul could say that, after his encounter with the cruciform faith, he counted all that he once valued as "crap" (*skybala*) in Philippians 3.

101

There is some tension within Scripture over the moral import of money. For instance, 1 Timothy warns that, "those who want to be rich fall into temptation and are trapped.... For the love of money is a root of all kinds of evil, and in their eagerness to be rich some have wandered away from the faith" (6:9-10). Yet the passage ends with a rather accommodated view of the rich within the church. "As for those who in the present age are rich, command them not to be haughty, or to set their hopes on the uncertainty of riches, but rather on God who richly provides.... They are to do good, to be rich in good works, generous, and ready to share, ... so that they may take hold of the life that really is life." (6:17-19).

When the rich young man is called to follow Jesus, he is commanded to give away all that he has to the poor. He went away "grieving" (Mark 10:22). We rich, Western Christians ought to take note that this is about the only time that Jesus invites someone to become his disciple and the person refuses—and the refusal was based upon riches.

By my reckoning, of the relatively sparse biblical ethical instruction for early Christian leaders, most is concerned with the perils of the love of money. Ironically, it is often the self-sacrificial attitude engendered by the faith of the cross that is sometimes cited as the excuse for clergy malfeasance: "My great sacrifices as a pastor justify my stealing." Of course, this is an abuse of the theology of the cross. Still, it is also a warning to us that we are often nowhere more self-deceptive than when we are dealing with money. In Acts 5:1-11, Peter accuses Ananias and Sapphira not of stealing (as I might have accused them), but rather of lying. There is a nice fit between our lies and our covetousness. All of this makes money a morally significant matter, particularly in light of the Christian faith's particular concern over riches.[5]

Richard Neuhaus's advice to new pastors is therefore biblically well taken:

> For many people, Sinclair Lewis's Elmer Gantry still casts a shadow of suspicion over Christian ministry. Journalists relentlessly press the Gantry syndrome in connection with very prominent ministers, eagerly sniffing about for that financial motive that "explains what he is really up to." Much of this is outrageously unfair, and yet it reflects a popular intuition about the connection between money and integrity that is not too far removed from the teachings of the gospels. Most of us do not "sell out" by making crooked deals, or even by consciously compromising principle in order not to compromise financial security; we pay our tribute to Mammon in the minutes and hours spent in worrying about money and the things that money can get.
>
> There are few decisions that a young pastor or pastoral couple make that are more important than the attitude toward money. One should as early as possible determine the top income one would ever want to strive to have. Of course there has to be a degree of flexibility in such a decision, but the question of money and the dangers it poses should be kept under the closest scrutiny. Otherwise the desire ineluctably grows, avarice feeds upon itself, and one ends up as the victim of an appetite that is in fact insatiable and consumes by worry, guilt, and discontent the hours and days that were once consecrated to ministry.[6]

Kierkegaard said, "The punishment I should like the clergy to have is a tenfold increase in salary. I am afraid that neither the world nor the clergy would understand this punishment."[7]

Those of us who minister in the affluent culture of North America are fortunate in not having to search for ways to be examples to our flocks. All we need to do is consider how we handle our money. Those clergy who justify their financial irresponsibility by saying, "I do not need to give money to the church because I give so much in so many other ways," are not only deceiving them-selves, but they are also presenting a horrible example to their congregations. Our giving to the church and its work ought to be exemplary in its effusiveness. We thereby not only demonstrate Christian stewardship in a society that encourages greed, but we also witness to the possibility that our lives and our possessions are not our own.

## NAILED TO THE CROSS

The bishop was complaining to me: "My younger pas-tors all seem to be stuck on the notion, 'I've got to look after me.' When they go to their first church, their first order of business is to attempt to negotiate a contract with the church, specifying days off and limits upon office hours. How does this morality square with service to a Master who said, 'Deny yourself'?"

As is any other Christian, a pastor is tethered to a cross. When Jesus mentioned leadership, telling us that our leading ought not to be like that of the Gentiles, I think he had most in mind our attachment to the cross. Such attachment flies in the face of much contemporary thought on human fulfillment. Jack L. Sammons Jr. has called our major modern ethical position, "rebellious ethics."[8] Rebellious ethics says that pastors, like other professionals, are most ethical when we stand apart from our professional roles in personal moral judgment of them. The worst moral danger, according to the para-digm of rebellious ethics, is for pastors to be captured by our professional roles. In other words, the goal of this ethic is to have no ethic imposed upon us by our role, to be the sort of pastor who can be a pastor without taking himself or herself too seriously, who can be more a per-son than a pastor. Or, as one pastor put it, "I'm a pastor, but sometimes I've got to lay that aside and just be myself."

The more we summon up the psychological courage to rebel against our socially imposed roles, the more ethical we will be, says rebellious ethics. The cynicism within the conversation of the Ministers' Monday Morning Coffee Hour, in which clergy sit around making cutting comments about their flocks or regale one another with sacrilegious jokes, represents a rather harmless attempt at ersatz rebellion from the clerical roles they find so confining, an attempt to deny clerical power by making fun of being a cleric. We clergy know enough about our roles to know that they put us in risky positions where power is being used and therefore potentially abused, but we don't know enough about how to change our professional practices to improve our profession.[9]

Rather than engage in deep reflection on the subtleties of the exercise of power in our roles, we sometimes adopt the stance of the romantic rebel, the fiction of the roleless person. Rebellious ethics assumes that it is the nature of all roles to undervalue the person as a *person* engaged in moral decision making. However, in deciding to fall back upon our own resources, to rebel against traditional expectations for pastors, we offer our people less rather than more. I agree that the worst possible advice you can give anyone is be yourself.

Ironically, in our determination to "just be myself" as we engage in pastoral work, we become examples of what Richard Rorty has called the Kantian divinized self. Having dethroned God, we become gods unto ourselves. Yet we are still not thereby free. Casting off the restraints of our clerical roles, asserting our individual personalities, we have not thereby rebelled against all external, socially assigned roles; rather, we fall backward into the clutches of the dominant cultural function of clergy in our day—the care, encouragement, and detachment of the individual psyche from any commitment other than dedication to the self.

As Martin Marty notes, American clergy function within a national polity in which the Constitution decreed early on in our national life that "religion had to be put in a legally subordinate situation in civil life, where so many ethical decisions are made."[10] By driving religion out of the public world into the private (as the Constitution tends to do to us), there was little of ethical importance (like politics or economics) left for religion to be ethical about, despite Marty's optimism that "to make religion legally subordinate does not mean that the State can render the clergy morally subservient."[11] The State, through the Constitution, has made individuals of us all, telling us that we have thereby been given the maximum amount of freedom through detachment from family, tradition, community, or history. The genius of this liberal constitutional arrangement is that, while telling us we are free, the modern State has discovered how much easier detached individuals are to manage than people who have a home, or a tribe, or a neighborhood, or a past.

Marty is right in his answer to his question, "What does this have to do with clergy ethics? It means that ministers...have the most direct effect on private and personal life. They have a measure of unimpeded influence on those who choose to affiliate with the religious body they serve. They also find themselves 'boxed in,' segregated as it were, in the private sphere. 'Religion is a private affair' is an effective way of cutting off the influence of clergy ethics.... To introduce a religious backdrop or argument appears to be an intrusion into the civil fabric."[12] The pastor compensates for this lack of public significance by becoming the eager chaplain to the dominant ethic: You stay out of my life and I'll stay out of yours. The "genius" of the contemporary pastor is that he

106

or she attempts to achieve public power by being nice—appearing to be caring, empathetic, and kind—while conveying this culture's official sanctioned ethic: There is no point to life other than that which you personally devise. You stay out of my life and I'll stay out of yours.

So in our willingness to keep things private and personal, detached from ecclesial demands, in exchange for our alleged religious freedom, clergy have not rebelled against cultural expectations. We have acquiesced into the most ethically debilitating of those expectations. It is not that we have been too good at being pastors and not good enough at being people; rather, we have not been good enough at being pastors. True morality—the ability to judge our own self-deception, the gift of seeing things in perspective—comes from practices outside those sanctioned by the system. It comes from being forced, Sunday after Sunday, to lead and to pray the Prayer of Confession followed by the Words of Absolution. It comes from being ordered, Sunday after Sunday, to "Do this in remembrance of me." In my case, it comes from being forced, Sunday after Sunday, to march in to church behind a cross, rather than behind a flag, my list of publications, or my pension portfolio.

Fortunately, there seems to be today a renewed stress upon spiritual disciplines, and the cultivation of those practices of prayer, meditation, and devotion that are gifts to all Christians, enabling us to persevere.

When I moved from parish ministry to campus ministry, I suddenly found a great need for some intentional, focused time, at the beginning of my workday, for devotion and reflection. For me this meant reading a group of collects from the *Book of Common Prayer* and praying a couple of the psalms before doing any other pastoral activity.

These acts of devotion helped to focus my work, served as a reminder to me of my peculiar identity as a priest in this academic setting, and gave me the authorization I needed to be on campus functioning not as a lower-level academic functionary, but as someone who looks for, points to, and talks about God. Such are the gifts of the spiritual disciplines.

Our extravagant claim is that through obedience to these crucial ("crucial" literally means *cross*) practices, Jesus gives us the resources we need to be faithful disciples. And we will never know whether or not Jesus was speaking truthfully if we pastors refuse to hold ourselves attached and accountable to Jesus' demands. Is the cross God's true way with the world or not? We shall never know unless we attempt to live lives based upon the cross.

During a recent lunch the chair of our chemistry department noted that ministers could profit by the ethics of chemists. "The ethics of chemists?" I asked. "Sure. It is impossible to be a good chemist and a liar at the same time. The chemist's honesty about experimental results, openness with other chemists, and commitment to standard methodology would enhance the practice of ministry." Which suggests that Jack Sammons is correct. We do not need to be better rebels from the virtues and practices of our craft; we need to be more deeply linked to them.

The irony in the practice of "rebellious ethics" is that by acting independently, thinking for ourselves, standing on our own two feet, we have not rebelled against the system; we have capitulated into its worst aspects. If we become separated from the skills and commitments of our craft, we are left morally exposed, victims of conventional wisdom. For pastors—particularly pastors who are also district superintendents, bishops, or denominational executives—the worst form of self-deception may be the deceptive idea that we are without power, that we are just "one of the boys or girls" and end up not taking ourselves seriously. We become simply a "person." Power ought to be owned, admitted, used responsibly, and critiqued publicly. The church is full of much harm done by powerful people who refuse to acknowledge how much they are able to hurt other people.

Consider again the virtues of preaching. The disciplines required by the craft of sermon preparation—self-criticism, obedience to the text, confidence in the congregation, weekly hard work—are disciplines that are more moral than technical or personal. In fact, that may be a good test for whether or not ordinands are morally ready to be entrusted with a congregation: Have they mastered the craft well enough to write fifty-two Sundays of sermons without lying too often?

The notion that we are most fully ourselves, most fully ethical when we have freed ourselves from the demands of Scripture, tradition, and church merely demonstrates the power of the socially sanctioned story that holds us captive. As George Lindbeck noted, we are all liberals. That is, the individual is the basic unit of reality, the sole center of meaning. We are all children of modernity, that story which holds that each of us has a right, a duty, to be free of all stories save the ones we have individually chosen. This is Peter Berger's "heretical imperative," the modern conceit that we are free to determine our own destinies, that we have no fate other than the fate we choose. In earlier times, heresy was that way of thinking in which a person chose what to believe rather than believed what he or she had been told. Today, we are all fated to be heretics in that we all live under the modern presupposition that none of us should be held to commitments that we have not freely chosen. Our morality has thus made freedom of choice an absolute necessity. Freedom has become the fate of the individual. If I explain my actions on the basis of tradition, community standards, my parents' beliefs, or Scripture, I have obviously not thought things through, have not decided for myself, have not been true to myself, have not rebelled against the external imposition of a role, so I have not been moral.

As Stanley Hauerwas has shown repeatedly, this mode of thinking is but another form of deception. Honesty ought to make modernity acknowledge that it is also enslaved to a story (the Enlightenment myth of the free individual) that tells us that it is possible to choose our own stories. We have merely exchanged narrative masters. We jettison the older, traditional story that it is my duty as an ordained leader of the church to bear the church's tradition before my congregation for a more socially acceptable one: My duty is to my individual feelings and standards in order to free my parishioners to be dutiful to their individual feelings and standards. The modern world said, That's only a story. The postmodern world has realized, There's only story. So the question is not, Shall our lives be narratively constructed? But, Which narrative shall form our lives?

Paul portrayed the cross as a great unmasker, a wonderful exposer of the powers. It is so difficult for modern liberal societies to acknowledge the subtle forms of coercion that hold them together because they derive their legitimization from the presumption that there is no moral authority more significant than the individual conscience. Believing this to be true, we dismiss Scripture, Jesus, church tradition, and the liturgy of the church in favor of the freedom to do what we think personally to be right. Yet such modes of thought can also be totalitarian. In America everyone is free to think whatever he or she wants, but everyone seems to think about the same.

Fortunately for us pastors, when we get personal, we get a personality upon whose head hands have been laid, around whose shoulders falls the yoke of Christ.

The question is never, "Shall I live my life on the basis of some external, socially imposed determination?" The only ethical question is, "Which externally imposed determination is worth my hope in life and in death?"

In a way, the externally imposed laying-on-of-hands gesture of ordination is a way of removing the matter of character from the realm of personal choice. Under orders, my life is no longer to be construed as the sum of my choices. Rather, my life is a process of discovering the significance of God's and the church's choice of me.

## SACRIFICES WORTH MAKING

Love of the gospel often throws us into conflict with other loves and loyalties. There is a kind of imperialism inherent in the gospel, an imperialistic determination to have all of us. In taking up the cross, we must deny something else. Self-denial is difficult enough. Denial of those most dear to us is worse. Cross produces conflict. When Chrysostom began to struggle with the idea of a call into the priesthood, his mother put great pressure upon him not to forsake her in her old age. His mother pleaded with Chrysostom to recall the sacrifices that she had made to ensure that he would be a well-provided-for, educated young man:

> Even when thou wast an infant, and hadst not yet learned to speak, a time when children are the greatest delight to their parents, thou didst afford me much comfort. Nor indeed can you complain that, although I bore my widowhood bravely, I diminished thy patrimony, which I know has been the fate of many who have had the misfortune to be orphans....I spared no expense which was needful to give you an honorable position, spending for this purpose some of my own fortune, and of my marriage dowry. Yet do not think that I say these things by way of reproaching you; only in return for all these benefits I beg one favor: do not plunge me into a

second widowhood; nor revive the grief which is now laid to rest: wait for my death: it may be in a little while I shall depart.... When, then, you shall have committed my body to the ground, and mingled my bones with thy father's, embark for a long voyage, and set sail on any sea thou wilt: then there will be no one to hinder thee: but as long as my life lasts, be content to live with me.[13]

I am not surprised to hear that pastors have a high degree of stress in their marriages and families. It is our peculiar burden to find our lives, like Chrysostom's, stretched between commitments to our mothers and mother church, our human families and the Family of God. The sacrifices that cause many pastors the most grief are not the sacrifices of material luxuries, but rather the sacrifices that they are forced to ask their families to make in order for pastors to follow their vocation. No general principles are helpful in these matters. There are times when our current stresses in ministerial marriages and family confirm the wisdom of the church's historic practice of clerical celibacy.

Allow me to say to those spouses and children who struggle with the demands placed upon them by a clergy parent or spouse that life could be worse. Every parent asks his or her children to suffer for the parent's values. Martin Luther is reputed to have said that whatever you would sacrifice your daughter for, that is your god. Many American families are sacrificing their sons and daughters upon the altar of rampant materialism and the wreckage of such sacrifice is all around us.

My wife's father was a United Methodist minister, as were her grandfather and grandmother. There was a time when she somewhat resented that, because of their work in the church, her parents were engaged so much of the time in church work and had little time for their children. However, as she later saw among some of her friends the burden of parents who have nothing more important to do in their lives than to live for their children, she saw what a gift her parents had given her in raising her in a parsonage family. Unlike some parents, her parents were not exclusively, selfishly turned in toward the interests of their family. They had the church. They made it clear to their children that others often had a claim upon their time and concern. They had something more important to do with their lives than simply give their lives for their biological children. They were members of a larger family called the church.

> Let goods and kindred go, this mortal life also; the body they may kill; God's truth abideth still; his kingdom is forever.[14]

The sacrifices demanded of clergy are worthwhile as sacrifices demanded by service to the truth who is Jesus Christ. The cross teaches us to have no qualms about suffering in service to the gospel. What is immoral is not one's suffering in service to the gospel, but rather one's suffering in service to triviality. What kills pastors is not service to the cause of Christ, for such service carries with it its own invigoration. What is so destructive is being asked to sacrifice marital happiness and family tranquillity, for those whose demanding self-centeredness has become an unbearable burden upon the pastor.

We pastors must examine our ministry—the way we spend our time, the way we use our talents—by asking ourselves, "Is this service to the cross of Christ or merely servitude to the omnivorous desires of North American discontented consumers?" Bishops and those who deploy clergy must not demean the sacrifice that is our call to the ministry by sending pastors to churches that have no mission and resist all efforts to find a mission. By justifying trivial, demeaning ministerial work with "you never know the good you may be doing there," or "surely something good may come out of this ministry, even though we cannot see it now" pastors degrade the significance of the pastoral vocation.

"It is not that pastors are not working hard," said one church official to me, "it is, rather, that too much of the work they do is hardly worth doing." Priorities must be set, time not wasted, talents not squandered, but none of this can happen unless pastors rest secure in the vocational conviction that what they do is authorized by God and necessary for the salvation of the world. It has been said that if pastors do not know what is absolutely essential in their ministry, they will do the merely important.

I know a pastor who called it quits by standing up without warning in a vestry meeting and announcing that he was leaving the priesthood. After the initial shock, an older member of the vestry asked, "Don't you think you owe us an explanation?"

He replied that he had entered the ministry to preach the gospel and to support the people of Christ in their discipleship. Yet over the years, his ministry had become little more than a boring matter of housekeeping and dull routine. He couldn't take it anymore, so he was leaving.

"Did it ever occur to you that many of us are bored too?" the church member persisted. "None of us have asked you to preach dull sermons. You do the things you do in ministry because that's what you do, not because we have demanded it. If you have some higher, more interesting and bold idea of what church ought to be, tell us. Some of us feel the same way you do about what this congregation's become."

With that began a discussion that continued well into the night concerning the point of the church, the purpose of ministry, and the message of the gospel. The priest stayed. The church was born again. Too many of us pastors too passively acquiesce into dull, theologically indefensible forms of ministry that trivialize our vocation, cause us to neglect our marriages and families, and ultimately lead to despair. One of the necessary pastoral tasks is forming congregations whose vision of the church gives dignity and validation to the sacrifices we make in being pastors.

A theology of the cross tends to be life-giving when applied to ourselves, but deadly when applied to the sacrifices made by others. Some feminist interpreters have been particularly critical of a theology of the cross when applied to women, saying that this theology has been used to underwrite the suffering of women in unjust social structures. The cross is placed upon the backs of all Christians, not just women, not just wives, not just clergy. I resonate with Ellen Charry's argument that the theology of the cross is a powerful force against male power abuse. Richard Hays has argued that any attempt to restrict the call to self-sacrificial crossbearing, to exempt women from the summons to take up the cross of Christ and follow Jesus, would be to patronize them by excusing them from the call to radical discipleship.[15]

Finally, I ought to mention that peculiar perversion of the theology of the cross that leads some clergy to think that because they have made certain sacrifices as pastors, this awards them an ethically exempt position in which the rules that are made for everyone else do not apply to them.

I recall with shame the layperson who told me about his discovery that his pastor had been stealing money from the church. The layperson was devastated by this discovery. Yet he was even more aghast by his pastor's justification that "this church has never adequately paid me for the time I give here. What you call 'theft' was only my just compensation."

While the sacrifices required of clergy are great and some of them are particular to being clergy, it is doubtful that they are any greater than the sacrifices required of any struggling disciple. All disciples are commanded to take up the cross, to throw away life for the sake of the gospel (Mark 8:34-35). What makes the sacrifices of clergy sometimes seem greater is some clergy's inclination to focus only on themselves, to assume that the challenges of their vocation are greater than those of others. Furthermore, submission to the way of the cross of Christ does not cancel out other ethical demands, but rather intensifies them in the light of Jesus' life and death.

Though the practice appears to be dying, I remember the day when clergy were often given discounts at golf courses, supermarkets, and other businesses because they were pastors. The practice surely stems from a time when pastors were universally poorly compensated and church members, who had little financial means themselves, often gave their pastor produce from their gardens or other goods and services as a means of showing gratitude and support for the pastor's ministry.[16]

In the light of most pastors' salaries, such discounts should not be accepted. Today this special treatment tends to demean the pastor's vocation and may be a way of inappropriately relieving some church members of their vocation to financially support their church.

## CONSTANCY

One of the most ethically significant aspects of preaching is disciplining oneself to preach texts prescribed by the Common Lectionary. We thereby demonstrate our subservience to the Word, preaching what we are told by the community of Christ to preach, not what we or our people at present may want to hear. In a culture that stresses liberation, freedom from all attachment, and rebellion against communal formation, it is important for clergy to demonstrate their attachment to the church. Our job is not to speak for ourselves as individuals, not primarily to share our personal feelings with our people. Our job is to demonstrate that lives ordered and ordained into the faith of the church are better than lives formed elsewhere.

American, evangelical Protestantism has tended to put too much stress upon feelings, affections, and sincerity as motivations for ethical behavior. Some of the best things that we preachers do, we do merely out of habit, because it's our job. So many of the tasks of ministry, over the long haul, are not personally invigorating. Boredom sets in. For those of us who have entered into the priesthood as a means of "personal fulfillment," or because "I like helping people," or some other essentially self-centered motivation, the dry valleys in ministry can be especially difficult. What we need is some means of ministry that keeps us at the tasks of *diakonia* even when we do not feel like it, even when we are not personally pleased to minister.

Jonathan Kozol spent a year living, working, and observing the mean streets of the South Bronx, the poorest neighborhood of America. He is not a religious man, but he wrote a book that is, among other things, a powerful testimony to the ministry there of St. Ann's Episcopal Church. One of the remarkable people in the book is Anthony, a twelve-year-old street kid who has managed to carve out an inspiring young life because of the protective embrace of St. Ann's. The pastor of the church, Martha Overall, left behind a career in law to lead the challenging ministry of St. Ann's. Kozol writes:

> The pastor rises at five A.M. She seldom seems to finish work much before ten at night. When people are sick, she takes them to the hospital. When their sons are arrested, she goes with them to court. When they are born, she baptizes them. This afternoon, I saw her with a wet mop

117

and a pail, washing the church floor...If she had remained a lawyer, she could be home now getting ready for dinner. I can see why Anthony feels safe when he is here.[17]

The evils of the world are too great, the people are too difficult. Noble, altruistic feelings are no match for the realities of Christian ministry in a fallen, not yet fully redeemed world. Therefore, I would now add *constancy* to the list of clerical virtues. Sunday keeps occurring even when we preachers don't feel like we want it to. There are great temptations to neglect those habits of study, sabbatical, and nurture that enable us to keep going.

In my own church, where we itinerate (move every few years), it is all too easy to ask for a move when our wells run dry. When we have nothing left to say, no more leadership to give at a congregation, it is too easy to say to the bishop, "Well, I think it's time for a move. I've done all the good I can do here."

What we mean is, "I have not the moral resources to dig down, to dig in, to retool, to go back to the wellsprings of inspiration through work, study, and prayer, and so I am going to move to another congregation rather than face my own need for renewal." One meets enough burned-out hulks at Annual Conference each year to serve as warnings to the rest of us of the perils of neglecting those habits that enable us to remain faithful and vital in ministry over the long haul.

Stanley Hauerwas says,

> I can think of no virtue more necessary to the ministry today than constancy. Without steadfastness to self and to one's task ministry cannot be sustained. Without constancy the minister is tempted to abandon the church to the ever-present temptation to unbelief and unbelief's most powerful ally, sentimentality. A minister must live and act believing God is present in the church creating, through word and sacrament, a new people capable of

witnessing to God's Kingdom. The minister must be filled with hope that God will act through word and sacrament to renew the church, but he or she must be patient, knowing that how God works is God's business. From the crucible of patience and hope comes the fidelity to task that makes the ministry not a burden but a joy.[18]

Constancy is a virtue based upon the theological conviction that God really is present in the church, in word and sacrament, even though that presence may not always be vivid in the experience of the moment, even though God may not operate on our timetable. Once, when I was asked, "What is the proof of Easter?" I responded, "The proof of Easter is that this Sunday, in a little crossroads in North Dakota, a preacher I know will stand in the pulpit and proclaim the grace of God in Christ even though in four years at this church none of her fifty parishioners has complimented her work or told her how much her ministry means to them." Clerical constancy is testimony to our faith in the ultimate triumph of the kingdom of God.

> Therefore, since we are justified by faith, we have peace with God through our Lord Jesus Christ, through whom we have obtained access to this grace in which we stand; and we boast in our hope of sharing the glory of God. And not only that, but we also boast in our sufferings, knowing that suffering produces endurance, and endurance produces character, and character produces hope, and hope does not disappoint us, because God's love has been poured into our hearts through the Holy Spirit that has been given to us. (Rom. 5:1-5)

Lest I speak too negatively of the burden of the cross, we ought to be reminded of Jesus' words that, when we take upon ourselves his yoke of obedience, his yoke is easy, his burden is light (Matt. 11:28-30). When is a burden light? It is when we find our burdensome lives caught up, elevated, borne aloft by something greater than our lives. Mission gives meaning. Jesus does not come to us to relieve us of all yokes or burdens; rather, he comes offering us a yoke worth wearing, a burden worth bearing. It is a great gift not to have to make your life mean something, to have your life given significance by the Lord whose cross, when taken up, takes us up as well.

It is in the context of the cross that we can examine what many have said is the greatest moral failing among ministers: sloth. In conversations with clergy administrators and those who supervise clergy, this is the sin that was most often mentioned—laziness, *acedia*, that noonday demon that afflicts those who no longer care and those for whom the fire has gone out and the light no longer shines. Busyness is not the same as work. Some very busy pastors are rushing around with calendars in hand and a full schedule of meetings and appointments before them, but are neglecting the essential tasks of ministry in favor of the merely important. This busyness is but another form of sloth that is called *distraction*.

Richard Hays begins his discussion of New Testament ethics by stressing the first ethical virtue not as some high-flown philosophical ideal, but as the basic virtue of "reading the text carefully"[19]; that is, work. Our need is not for a better set of "values," those limp, insubstantial lists of ideals that have little discernible effect on our lives. Our need is for good habits, for commitment to certain tasks that keep us faithful. We need to keep at it. I believe the roots of clerical sloth are theological rather than primarily psychological. We become lazy and slovenly in our work because we have lost a rationale for the work.

A bishop noted that in every case in his episcopacy where there was a pastor who was guilty of laziness, he found a pastor who had lost a compelling sense of vocation. Any pastor who feels deeply called to be in ministry will find the means to do it. A pastor who has lost a sense of vocation will find even the slightest ministerial tasks to be great drudgery. Therefore this book began, you will recall, with a discussion of vocation as the wellspring of pastoral morality.

The call to constancy is why we must preach cross and resurrection together. We are able to take up the cross, to keep at the challenges of Christian ministry, because we consider the cross from the perspective of Easter. The ultimate triumph of God, God's vindication of the way of the cross, was demonstrated in the resurrection. Knowledge of that ultimate triumph keeps us taking up the cross, keeps us at ministry even when we are not given visible results, even when it is not personally fulfilling to prepare sermons, to visit the sick, to tend the body of Christ. Because of our conviction of God's *hesed,* God's "steadfast love," as the Scriptures call it, we are able, despite ourselves, to be steadfast. God keeps coming back for us, keeps with us, even when we fail to keep with God. Our ministerial constancy is but a reflection of God's constancy toward us, constancy that we name as Jesus Christ. As John Howard Yoder puts it, the cross "is the kingdom come" in which our heuristic focal images of community, cross, and resurrection are brought together. The church should be known, Yoder says, by "an ethic marked by the cross, a cross identified as the punishment of a man who threatens society by creating a new kind of community leading a radically new kind of life."[20] In the next chapter, when we examine the ministerial need for Sabbath, we shall note the curious linkage between sloth and overwork, both of which are sometimes tied to an inadequate theology of the gracious activity of a resurrected Lord.

Before leaving the issue of constancy I feel compelled to note that in some cases, the most ethically responsible act for some pastors is for them to cease being pastors, to leave the pastoral ministry and to assume some other form of Christian ministry. Conversations with bishops and others in authority over pastors have convinced me that we must challenge the medieval notion that one is "a priest forever," once a priest, always a priest. Again, pastors are significant, not because of some inner, ontological essence they possess, but rather because of what needs to happen in the church. A functional rather than an ontological basis of the priesthood is essential. When a pastor is no longer effective and helpful to the mission of the church as a pastor, the honorable thing is for that pastor to remove himself or herself from the pastoral ministry.

One bishop told me that, in his opinion, this was the greatest need in the church today: for judicatory officials who care enough about pastors and their churches to help ineffective pastors out of the pastoral ministry. Sloth and patterns of negligence are often sure signs that one has lost a sense of vocation. Without great guilt or shame, pastors who have lost a vocation ought to be compassionately helped into another line of work. We ought to honor those pastors who have the love of the church and the respect for the vocation of ministry to say, "I have given my best to this calling for the past twenty years. Now I need to find another vocation."

## THE PERILS OF A THEOLOGY OF GLORY

Many of us have encountered a remarkably similar story in our ministries. There was a "golden boy" (for the sake of the story let's assume it was indeed a boy) in your seminary class, someone who seemed to win all the preaching awards, write the most theologically astute papers, and get the most attention from the professors. After graduation he moved quickly through his apprenticeship positions, always winning the approval of his mentors and denominational overseers. Now, a few years later, he's shown up in your town, senior pastor of the largest congregation in your denomination. He's the youngest person ever to hold the position. It's a comfortable, affluent suburban church, with a membership of well-educated professionals. They expect their pastor to preach and teach an urbane, sophisticated version of the faith. Your former classmate doesn't let them down.

The word on the street is that things are going well at the big church. New programs are springing up left and right, the congregation is growing, and the pastor is frequently asked to represent the clergy at civic events. He always seems to be on the golf course, in the company of folks whose golf clubs and bags cost more than your car. If he hasn't seemed to strike up many friendships with other pastors, personal jealousy is the obvious reason. His church often gains members at the expense of other congregations in the community, which has to be why the other clergy are having such a hard time liking or trusting him.

When people talk about his preaching, it is almost always in glowing terms, applauding his skill in addressing contemporary issues (without, it seems, ever stepping on anyone's toes), and especially his professional manner in the pulpit. Once or twice, however, you've heard a different response. A couple of folks have said, "You know, it's kind of hard to get a read on what he thinks about being a Christian. When he talks about the church he grew up in, it's usually to put it down. He often says something about what other Christians think, and you get the feeling that he thought that way too, once, but now he's grown out of it. I guess the folks in his church like to think they've grown out of their childish faith, too."

As the years progress he moves in ever-widening circles of influence, and his preaching takes on more of the mocking tone that you've heard about. Everything he says comes from a standpoint of superiority, as though his task were not to defend the faith, but rather to point out its follies and foibles. Even some of his own members have noticed, although none of them have felt they could say anything, given the large numbers of his approving admirers. More often than before you hear folks wonder about why he spends little time with the biblical text in his sermons.

Soon the whispers start, whispers about behavior that could be construed as inappropriate. You notice that he seems to be extremely busy, always showing up at this or that denominational or community gathering. You wonder if he ever spends any time in the office, or at the hospital. When you see him he seems to be in a constant adrenaline rush. His smile is expansive, his voice is booming, he asks about your ministry, listening carefully to what you say, shaking his head appreciatively at all the right moments...yet the light of attention has flickered out in his eyes.

Then, one day, it all comes crashing down. He's had an affair (probably with the wife of someone on his staff), word of it comes to light, and he's been asked to resign. He will have to go through some kind of formal or informal period of penance. He might have to leave the ordained ministry altogether, although that is becoming less and less the rule. His church is deeply wounded; many of the members drift away disillusioned, never to return there or to any other congregation.

As you and your clergy colleagues perform your postmortems, there is the usual mix of "How the mighty have fallen!" and "There, but for the grace of God, go I." Yet in the back of your mind there's another thought, one that you might have shared with your peers, but probably not. "Why," you ask yourself, "am I not surprised? He had everything going for him; he was on track to be bishop. It seems unbelievable that he would have self-destructed, yet I have no problem believing it at all. Why is that?"

Could it be because of what you knew about his preaching? On the face of it, the possibility seems absurd. To be certain, you thought that his preaching had become less and less faithful to the gospel. Yet to say that bad preaching and adultery reveal one and the same failure of character is surely to commit an egregious leap of logic. Or is it? Is it so hard to believe that someone who would preach the faith in order to free people from it is just the sort of person who would be unfaithful in his marriage? Why is infidelity to the vow we took at ordination to rightly explain the word of truth so different from infidelity to the vow we took at marriage to forsake all others, being faithful to our spouse? The answer to these questions can only be made in reference to the peculiar character of clergy.

That such a claim seems absurd may show how little we respect the power of preaching. If we will not be subservient to the Word, if we will not preach what the church has ordained us to preach, if we will not be tethered to the cross, we shall serve and be tethered to some god or other good. Let this narrative and the similar ones that have arisen in your experience be a reminder to us of the perils of poor preaching.

Luther was fond of contrasting a "theology of glory," in which the cross was seen as avoidable, optional equipment for Christians, with a "theology of the cross" which, according to Luther, calls things by their proper names and is unimpressed with most that impresses the world. To bear the cross of Christ is to bear its continual rebuke of the false gods to which we are tempted to give our lives. "Autosalvation" is the lie beneath most theologies of glory.

Yet to take up the cross of Christ, to be willing to

assume a yoke of obedience upon our shoulders, oblivious to the praise or blame of our congregations, is also the basis of what it means to have life and that abundantly, to live one's life in the light of true glory come down from heaven in the person of Jesus the Christ.

# CHAPTER FIVE

# *New Creation*

Paul was stunned by the reality of the resurrection—the way God not only vindicated Jesus by raising him from the dead, but also thereby recreated the whole *kosmos*. In Easter, an old world had terminated and a new one was being born, so Paul was forced to rethink everything that he had previously thought, including ethics. Much of what Paul says about Christian behavior was formed as his testimony to the resurrection, an event that he had experienced within the dramatic turnaround in his own life. Yet there was nothing merely subjective in Paul's vocation.[1] The call of Paul the apostle was his experience of finding himself living in a whole new world. He changed because of his realization that, in Jesus Christ, the world had changed. Paul's key testimonial to this recreation is in his Second Letter to the Corinthians:

> So if anyone is in Christ, there is a new creation: everything old has passed away; see, everything has become new! All this is from God, who reconciled us to himself through Christ, and has given us the ministry of reconciliation. (2 Cor. 5:17-18)

Verse 17, in the Greek, lacks both subject and verb so it is best rendered by the exclamatory, "If anyone is in Christ—new creation!"

Certainly, old habits die hard. There are still, as Paul acknowledges so eloquently in Romans 8, "the sufferings of this present time" (v. 18). The resistance and outright rejection that many women pastors suffer are evidence that the church has not yet fully appreciated the eschatological, end-of-the-age, transformed social arrangements that ought to characterize the church. That many ministers base their ministry on models of leadership uncritically borrowed from the latest fads in business or other secular leadership practices is yet another testimony to our failure to believe that God raised Jesus Christ from the dead, thus radically changing everything. It makes a world of difference whether or not one knows about the resurrection. Thus, making doxology to God (Rom. 11:33-36), Paul asks that we present ourselves as "a living sacrifice, holy and acceptable to God" by not being "conformed to this world" but by being "transformed by the renewing of your minds" (Rom. 12:1-2). All of this is resurrection talk, the sort of tensive situation of those who find their lives still in an old, dying world, yet who also are conscious of a new world being born. Our lives are eschatologically stretched between the sneak preview of the new world being born among us in the church and the old world where the principalities and powers are reluctant to give way. In the meantime, which is the only time the church has ever known, we live as those who know something about the fate of the world that the world does not yet know.

Thus Allen Verhey, in his examination of New Testament ethics, says that the key to everything ethical in the New Testament is "the resurrection of the crucified Jesus of Nazareth." Verhey contends that this is not merely an ethically significant aspect of the good news, it is "the basis and at the center of the New Testament," the "prism" through which "all sources of moral wisdom must pass."[2] Knowing the end, that is, the *telos* of this world that is being birthed into God's intentions, we are those who have been called "that... we might become the righteousness of God" (2 Cor. 5:21). Richard Hays notes that this is a rather amazing statement. We, being "in Christ" and being made a "new creation," are those who don't just know about the righteousness of God, or believe in the righteousness of God; we are to *be* God's righteousness.[3] If you want a scriptural basis for Christian ethics, make it this one. We are those who are called to be none other than the very embodiment of the righteousness of God in the world.

The expectations of pastors might seem unrealistic or hopelessly idealistic were it not for the resurrection. We are not our own. When, at the end of the Gospel of Matthew, Jesus tells us to go into all the world, making disciples, baptizing, and teaching, he rescues us from despair by his concluding promise that he is always with us, even to the end of the age (Matt. 28:20).[4] Our obedience is made possible through his presence. With all Christians we take confidence in the promise that "God... is at work in you, enabling you both to will and to work for his good pleasure" (Phil. 2:13). Paul gathers up all three of our focal images—community, cross, and resurrection—in a passage from Philippians in which he internalizes the resurrection and makes Easter the source of his own continuing struggle to be faithful:

> I want to know Christ and the power of his resurrection and the community of his sufferings by becoming just like him in his death, so that I might be like him in his resurrection. No, I have not already obtained such a state, nor have I already reached the goal; but I press on to make it my own, because Christ Jesus has made me his own. Sisters and brothers, I do not consider that I have

already made this my own; but this one thing I do: forgetting what lies behind and straining forward toward what lies ahead, I press on toward the goal, the prize, the upward call of God in Jesus Christ. (Phil. 3:10-14, my translation)

## HUMOR

How can one read the resurrection narratives without being impressed by their humor? Among the most astounded and disbelieving of the resurrection are Jesus' own disciples. Even when the risen Christ takes time to explain everything to them, they fail to get it (Luke 24:13-27). I love John's laconic comment that, after witnessing the spectacular first Easter, the empty tomb and all, "Then the disciples returned to their homes" (John 20:10). They went home! These were the sort of folk who could witness a resurrection and then go back to business as usual. If an early church father's characterization of Easter as "the joke that God played on the Devil" is true, then most of his disciples, at least at the first, did not get the joke. In a way, Easter keeps on being God's great joke played on the despair and the prudence of a church more willing to believe in Good Friday than in Easter.

Those who have kept at the Christian ministry longer than I will confirm the essential virtue of humor. One can be a pastor with only modest intellectual abilities, but one cannot remain a pastor for long without a sense of humor.[5] The ability to laugh at life's incongruities, to take God seriously but not ourselves, to embrace the strangeness of our people instead of strangling them to death with our bare hands is great grace. Without humor, a bishop could be an insufferable bore, a district superintendent could be dangerous, and a pastor would be in a perpetual state of depression due to the state of the church. Humor is the grace to put our problems in perspective, to sit lightly upon our clerical status, to be reminded that Jesus really did need to save us, seeing as we have so little means to save ourselves. Humor is just a glimpse, on a human scale, of the way God looks upon us from God's unfathomable grace. As has often been said, the essence of sin is to take ourselves too seriously. Forgiveness and humor appear to be close kin, certainly humor is quite close to grace.

There is a close connection between the disruptive quality of humor and Jesus' primary means of communication, the parable. John Dominic Crossan demonstrated how Jesus' parables assault rather than establish a "world."[6] A parable typically takes the predominant, officially sanctioned view of reality within a given culture, the "world," and then subverts that world. The surprise endings of many parables are close cousins to the endings of jokes. The gospel, in order to make its way in the world, must subvert the received world. Because pastors, if they are half faithful, must be forever challenging the received world of their people. Effective pastors are often masters at irony, satire, and other forms of linguistic subversion.

Some pastors are, by their very existence, parables that challenge the world's story of what is going on in the world. "I love my pastor," said an enthusiastic undergraduate. "He is your typical, perfect pastor, always late for meetings, office always a wreck, books and papers all over the front seat of his car. He called me last night after midnight to see how I was getting along in college."

I wondered at the effect of this pastor—one so full of disorder and procrastination—upon this punctilious, precise, orderly undergraduate. Perhaps his raucous life hints to her of the possibility of a more gracious, less driven existence.

I suppose that humor is a gift, yet I also believe that it is a gift that, even if modestly bestowed, can be cultivated. The cultivation of humor is a matter of constant attentiveness to the incongruities between God's will and our own, God's intent for Creation and the world's will for itself. Scripture is a great help. I recommend frequent forays into the Gospel of John.[7] There, the people around Jesus, the beneficiaries of his instruction, hardly ever get the point. Corpses are raised from the dead and water turns to wine just by his presence. Hardly anyone is able to get a handle on Jesus, so to speak, just like Mary Magdalene tried literally to do at Easter (John 20:17). When some doubt that he has been resurrected, Jesus responds by asking them if they have any fish for breakfast (21:5).

John is therefore a wonderful antidote to the hypnotic power of the ordinary. Just the sort of Gospel for pastors who have allowed their ministry to degenerate into mere maintenance. As a Christian communicator, I love the way John is willing to have us misunderstand his Gospel, allowing us to not get the point. In so many Johannine passages, even after our skillful interpretation, there are still aspects yet to be explained, there is still a surplus of meaning that is not exhausted by our interpretation. John seems to feel that there ought to be some distance maintained between us and the throne of God. Humor, when it is holy, gives God room to be God and not our self-derived conception. We priests help to mediate God to our people, but we must not make God so accessible that God is no longer God.

The humble distancing that is engendered by humor can be a great gift to the pastor's role of biblical interpreter within the congregation. Biblical interpretation today is susceptible to the sin of modern arrogance. Much of historical criticism begins from some preconceived modern framework, a prior judgment about what can and cannot be received by the "modern mind." Modernity assumes that all mystery is only a matter of temporary ignorance of due causes, assumes that it is possible for us to grasp everything we seek to understand. The modern world has a nasty habit of assuming that its "world" is a fact to be accepted rather than a social construction to be questioned. The biblical critic first takes some prickly, difficult-to-contain biblical text, dissects the text, contextualizes it in some alleged historical setting, demands that a text submit to modern laws of what can and cannot happen, then explains the text to us so the text no longer surprises.

There is a kind of blasphemy lurking behind the homiletical temptation to stand in the pulpit and explain the Bible to our people, to make everything accessible to our congregations, once biblical truth has been forced through our interpretive filters. We thus diffuse potentially explosive biblical texts, render them accessible to everyone, explain them, reduce them to that which can be comprehended by the limited but still arrogant "modern mind," and everyone nods in agreement with the sermon and then files out for lunch.

It takes great faith in Easter, particularly faith in the gift of the Holy Spirit, to be honest with our people that we have not a clue to the meaning of some biblical passage, or that we have no sense of a satisfying ending for a sermon, or that we are unsure of precisely what the congregation ought to do after hearing a given text. The most ethically dangerous time within a sermon is toward the end of the sermon, when we move from proclamation to application and act as if we know more than God. Sometimes we preachers are tempted to play God, to fill all the gaps between Jesus and our people, to make Christ too easily available to them, to dumb down discipleship. "Stewards of God's mysteries" (1 Cor. 4:1) ought not be too free in dispensing and disposing of the mystery that is Christ. We ought to preach in such a way that, if Jesus has not been raised from the dead, then our sermons are utterly incomprehensible. Faithful sermons require the presence of the Holy Spirit to make them work.

That dear, departed resident alien among us, William Stringfellow, said it so much more eloquently than I, with his words, with his life:

> To know the Word of God in the Bible, a [person] must come to the Bible with a certain naïveté, confessing that if God exists at all, [God] lives independently, though not in isolation, from [anyone's] intelligence, longing, emotion, insight or interpretations, even those which divine the truth. [One] must be open to God's initiative. [One] must be bereft of all preconceptions...surrender all [one's] own initiative....[One] must take the appalling risk....When a [person] is so naked, so helpless, so transparent, when [one] so utterly ceases to try to justify [oneself] or anyone or anything else, [one] first becomes vulnerable to the Word of God....When a [person] becomes that mature as a human being he [or she] is freed to listen and at last to welcome the Word...[and] is enlightened to discern the same Word of God at work now in the world....Thus is established a rhythm in the Christian's life encompassing [a person's] intimacy with the Word of God in the Bible and [one's] involvement with the same Word active in the world.[8]

Aristotle noted that there is more than a touch of aggression in much humor. Humor can be a means of self-justification as we put down others in order to build up ourselves. Yet self-deprecating humor, especially among clergy who are often encouraged to take ourselves with a seriousness that is deadly, can be a form of repentance. In humor's playful light, our achievements are less impressive than we make them out to be. Our failures are also less impressive. Humor can be the joke that God plays upon our sin, an expression of the experience of forgiveness. To take God a bit more seriously and ourselves a bit less so is a font from which flow not only most good jokes, but also much faithful clerical morality.

## DESPAIR AS SIN

Because of Easter, we are not permitted despair. There is certainly enough failure and disappointment in the church to understand why depression, disillusionment, and despair could be considered the three curses of pastoral ministry. Despair is most understandable among some of our most visionary and dedicated pastors. Any pastor who is not tempted by despair has probably given in to the world too soon, has become too easily pleased by and accommodated to present arrangements. Daily confrontation with the gap between who God has called the church to be and what the church actually is leads many of our best and brightest to despondency. We grieve for the church. Yet, as Paul says, we do not grieve as those who have no hope. If our hope were in ourselves or our techniques for the betterment of the church, we might well abandon all hope. Our hope is in Christ, who for reasons known only fully to himself, has determined the church as the major form of his visible presence in the world. Many days I do not know why, and many days I see no evidence for such faith in us. Yet by the grace of God, I do so believe. In Jesus Christ, God is reconciling the world to himself. And Easter tells us that God's purposes shall not be defeated, not by Satan, or death, or principalities and powers, or even by the church itself.

There is that sort of pastoral despair that leads some of our brothers and sisters to quit. Yet there is also that despair, which I find more widespread, that leads some of us to slither into permanent cynicism about the church. In my efforts to reform and to renew my own denomination, I at first thought that much of the resistance I encountered was due to the conservative, reactionary ways of leaders of the church. The powerful always tend to protect the status quo, to preserve the power arrangements that put them in their place, saying "We have never done it that way."

Upon further reflection, I saw some of their resistance to change as being due to the cynical belief that we cannot change, that God either will not or cannot do any new thing with us. It is sad to see accommodation to sin and death. How do we know that Easter is not true? Who told us that Jesus used bad judgment when he made us his resurrection witnesses even to the ends of the earth?

Christian ethics can never be a matter of mere avoidance of certain activity. It must also be characterized by enthusiastic (literally, filled with the divine), hopeful engagement and action. The willingness to settle down into merely present arrangements, to keep house, to maintain the status quo is a sin against Sunday. Our mainline Protestant willingness to see our churches decline, to be sociologically determined out of existence, not to let go of the old and embrace the new, not to put new wine into new wineskins, is not simply boring and uncreative, it is unfaithful.

In J. F. Powers's novel, *The Wheat That Springeth Green*, an old, overworked priest is finally sent a curate to help him care for his parish. The curate cannot type, does not keep regular office hours, and is no help in the old priest's attempt to climb out of the mire of his horribly boring, humdrum round of priestly duties. The old priest explains reality to the young curate. Sweeping his hand across the expanse of the cluttered office, he rages, "This—*all* this—isn't my idea of the priesthood. But this is how it is, Bill, and how it's going to be. This is *it*, Bill—the future. I'm sorry."[9]

In order for the powers-that-be to have their way with

us, to convince us that the rumor of resurrection is a lie, they must first convince us that death is "reality," and that wisdom comes in uncomplaining adjustment to that reality—"This is *it.*"

The theologian Jürgen Moltmann, once said that if one considers the evidence for the resurrection of Jesus, it is difficult to see why anyone would disbelieve it, except for two reasons: The resurrection is an odd occurrence, outside the range of our usual experience, so that makes it difficult for our conceptual abilities. Perhaps more important, if Jesus is raised from the dead, then we must change. Resurrection carries with it a claim, a demand that we live in the light of this stunning new reality. Now we must either join in God's revolution or else remain unchanged, in the grip of the old world and its rulers, sin and death.

Thus because we preachers must, at least on a yearly basis, preach resurrection, we keep being challenged to minister in the light of the resurrection. We are not permitted the old excuse for lethargy, "people don't change." Certainly, everything we know about people suggests that they usually don't change. But sometimes they do. Change is rare; indeed it would be considered virtually impossible were it not that Jesus has been raised from the dead. When a pastor keeps working with some suffering parishioner even when there is no discernible change in that person's life or when a pastor keeps preaching the truth even with no visible congregational response, that pastor is being a faithful witness to the resurrection (Luke 1:2). That preacher is continuing to be obedient to the charge of the angel at the tomb to go and tell something that has changed the fate of the world (Matt. 28:7).

I love that incident in Luke when, after Jesus has sent out the Seventy to preach, to heal, and to próclaim peace—in short, to do the same ministry that he himself has been doing—the Seventy "return with joy" (Luke 10:17). It works! We are actually ministers! "In your name even the demons submit to us!"

Jesus breaks into their report with, "I watched Satan fall from heaven like a flash of lightning" (10:18). In other words, this ministry is much more than helping people, more even than healing or preaching. Something grand, sweeping, and cosmic is being worked out through us and our work. This is bigger than we imagined. God is taking back the whole cosmos through our faithful work. We are not only fulfilling the task assigned to us by the bishop, our "names are written in heaven" (10:20). What we tend to think of as the humdrum tasks of ministry are in reality a kind of cosmic war:

> For our struggle is not against enemies of blood and flesh, but against the rulers, against the authorities, against the cosmic powers of this present darkness, against the spiritual forces of evil in the heavenly places. (Eph. 6:12)

There is thus something inherent in the practice of ministry that keeps Christian ministry predisposed toward expectation of miracle, surprise, and change. Easter ought to make us more persistent, more willing to engage in recklessness derived from our anticipation of the future. Lacking the empowerment provided by the resurrection, we are always in danger of falling back upon common sense, what is "realistic" or "responsible." Easter people ought to be more foolish than that.

After viewing the Robert Duvall movie, *The Apostle,* my wife's Bible study group discussed the implications of the movie.

"I didn't like the movie because I didn't like the minister," said one. "He was such a scoundrel—adulterer, liar, then murderer."

"But that's just the point," said another. "Look at all

the good, beautiful things God did through such a person."

"Well, maybe," persisted the other. "I still think that is a scandal for someone like that to be presented as a minister. I think of pastors as more holy and good than that."

I flinched when my wife said, "I suppose you haven't been around that many ministers, have you?"

All of the moral requirements for clergy are undertaken against the backdrop of the constant confession of sin and the constant pronouncement for forgiveness of sins that is the Sunday worship of the church. Paul was not only the great missionary to the Gentiles but also living proof that the dead can be raised, thus accounting for his frequently self-referential testimonials of his encounter with Christ. In that encounter, the dead Jesus was not only seen as raised, but the church enemy number one was also raised. On Easter, Jesus was not just raised from the dead and returned to faithful followers; he returned to us though we were the very ones who had so forsaken and denied him. When he appeared first and most frequently to his own disciples, the very ones who, when the soldiers came to arrest him had fled into the darkness, the risen Christ thereby demonstrated that it is the nature of the true and living God to forgive.

So the pastor tends to receive the elements of the Eucharist first, because the pastor is the chief of sinners. We need not self-deceive, excuse, or attempt to explain away our failures to live up to the demands of our ministerial vocation. We do not have to because we have been, are being, and will be forgiven. Preaching is weekly training in the art of asking and receiving forgiveness. Nearly every sermon I preach ought to be preceded by a paraphrase of Jesus: "Lord, forgive me, I do not know what I do."

When we fail as pastors, it is good to look for the opportunity to ask for the forgiveness, not only of God, but also of our congregations. We thus demonstrate that the church is the community of the forgiven and the forgivers. We model for our members the dynamic of confession and forgiveness, repentance and restoration that ought to characterize the Christian life. That which saves Christian ethics from being heroic, impossible, or even cruel for those who attempt to practice them, is the reckless forgiveness of a God who keeps taking us back even when we do not deserve it.[10]

Easter keeps differentiating the church from a respectable, gradually progressive, moral improvement society. Here, there are sudden lurches to the left and to the right, falling backward and lunging forward. Easter keeps reminding us pastors that the church is the result of something that God in Jesus Christ has done, not something we have done. This reminder is great grace to those well-disciplined, hard-working, conscientious pastors who are so often in danger of thinking that the kingdom of God depends mostly on them. Easter is also a warning to cautious and too prudent pastors that they ought to expect to live on the edge, ought not to expect to be "kept" by the church, that God seems to enjoy shocking and surprising those who think that they are tight with God. We therefore ought to press the boundaries of what is possible and what is impossible in ministry. We ought to keep working the edges as if miracles were not miraculous at all but simply typical of a God who loves to raise the dead. We ought to minister in such a reckless, utterly-dependent-upon-God sort of way that, if God has not vindicated the peculiar way of Jesus by raising him from the dead, then our ministry is ridiculous.

## SABBATH

In its narrative of the gift of the Decalogue to Israel, Exodus expends more verses on the command related to the Sabbath than on any other. The Sabbath is there first presented as a matter of our imitation of God. God rested on the seventh day, so ought we. There is a sense in which all the commandments of the Decalogue flow from the third commandment. All of the commandments are liturgical before they are ethical, a means of worship, of praising God with our lives. Sabbath is the means by which true worship is possible, whereby we are commanded to take the time that is required for the reflection, remembrance, and rest that is the prerequisite for faithful, responsive action in praise of God.

Sabbath keeping is a visible witness to the truth of the new creation begun in the resurrection of Christ. Sabbath is a publicly enacted sign of our trust that God keeps the world, therefore we don't have to. God welcomes our labors, but our contributions to the world have their limits. Our taking of responsibility is always reflexive, responsive to God's prior actions. Since God trusted creation enough to be confident that the world would continue while God rested, so should we. Unlike the Greek god Atlas, we need not bear the world on our shoulders. Like God, we can stay away from the office for a day of rest in the conviction that the world will not go to hell simply because we are not there to run the world.

It may seem odd to speak of resting and doing nothing as ethical activities. Yet consider how much havoc has been wreaked in the world due to our ceaseless work and striving. We get organized, make plans, move forward, begin to build. Babel is frequently the result of human busyness (Gen. 11). Thus Thomas Merton once spoke of our overwork as a form of violence against God's gift of rest. On the Sabbath we stop and take stock. We find ourselves falling back upon the Everlasting Arms, resting upon the promises of God not to desert us, not to allow chaos to overwhelm. It takes a people confident in God to rest.

Karl Barth opens his extended discussion of Christian Ethics with consideration of the holy day:

> The Sabbath commandment explains all the other commandments, or all the other forms of the one commandment. It is thus to be placed at their head. By demanding man's abstention and resting from his own works, it explains that the commanding God, who has created man and commissioned him to do his work, is the God who is gracious to man in Jesus Christ. Thus it points him away from everything that he himself can will and achieve and back to what God is for him and will do for him. It reminds man of God's plan for him, of the fact that He has already carried it out, and that in His revelation He will execute both His will with him and His work for him and toward him. It points him to the Yes which the Creator has spoken to him, his creature, and which He has continued and at last definitely acknowledges, which He has made true and proved true once and for all in Jesus Christ.[11]

Sabbath rest testifies to the complete goodness of God's creativity. As Barth says, "In deference to God, to the heart and meaning of his work, there must be from time to time an interruption, a rest, a deliberate non-continuation, a temporal pause, to reflect on God and His work and to participate consciously in the salvation provided by Him to be awaited from Him."[12]

Christians believe that Sabbath has been forever changed through the resurrection. Jesus was raised on the eighth day, becoming for us a new creation, giving us back time in a way we would not have had without God's raising Jesus from the dead. Just as God entrusted to Israel the Sabbath so that the world might know God's intentions for creation, so Christians worship on the day of the resurrection, thereby signaling that God's promise to Israel has gone to all the world. All are created to share the rest, the salvation, that comes from worship of the true God, including pastors.

It is therefore an ethical challenge that pastors must work on Sunday, the Christian Sabbath. While we are urging our people to pause, to remember, to reflect, to experience God's recreation of their lives on the eighth day, we clergy are busy speaking, leading, preaching, teaching, and presiding. This means that pastors must find some means of Sabbath since, in our peculiar vocation, Sabbath is often denied us because of our offering Sabbath to everyone else on Sunday. It is crucial for pastors to carve out some means of Sabbath as a witness that God, not pastors, preserves the church.

Sunday is the key that explains to the world and to the church why we are the church. In our Sunday worship Christians serve the world by showing the world that God has not left us alone and that we have good work to do. Our work is worship. Liturgy means in its Greek derivation, "the work of the people." Worship is the work God does with us to show the world a manner of life that could not be known had not God vindicated Jesus in the resurrection. Sabbath is a weekly reminder that we are created for no better purpose than to praise God and to enjoy God forever.

In simply withdrawing from what the world considers its "important business," in taking time to do nothing but worship in a world at war, in celebrating an "order of worship" in a world of chaos, Christians are making a most "political" statement. It takes courage to take time to worship God in a world where we are constantly told that it is up to us to do right, or right won't be done. Sunday is that holy time when Christians perform one of our most radical, countercultural, peculiarly defining acts—we simply refuse to show up for work. Sabbath is how we put the world in its place. This is how we take over the world's time and help to make it God's time. It's how we get over our amnesia and recover our memory of how we got here, and who we are, and in whose service we are called. Memory is hard for us, not because we must resuscitate in memory a dead Jesus, but rather because we become distracted from the joyful truth that Jesus is resurrected, present among us in time, for all time. Sabbath is a time for remembrance. Extracted from the daily, pressing, relentless cares and concerns of the parish, the pastor is given the opportunity for reflection and recollection, recalling why we are in ministry in the first place, to whom we are ultimately accountable, and where our ministry is meant to be heading.

The Sabbath is one of the church's most "political" acts. Christian politics is constituted by the worship of the true God found in Jesus Christ. It is politics that assumes that we have all the time in the world, eternity, in a world of deep injustice and pain, to take time to worship. In an unjust world, we either want anxiously to take time into our hands and right the wrong on our terms, or worse, to acquiesce to the injustice, giving it sovereignty, assuming that God cannot or will not work in time to do a new thing. Sunday worship is thus a radical protest from the world's time, a time when we literally take time to rejoice that in Jesus Christ, God has made our time God's own. We are given on the Sabbath a glimpse of eternity, an experience of what God means for all time where God has "blessing and honor and glory and might forever and ever!" (Rev. 5:13).

An overworked, busy and distracted, family-neglecting pastor is often a pastor with an inadequate theology of the resurrection. We are free to let go of the church, free to take regular sabbatical, because we rest in the conviction that Christ really is present in the church, that Christ will preserve the church and that the gates of hell, or even our day off, will not defeat the church. We have been created, not for ceaseless activity, but for rest, for confident Sabbath. Since our God was so serenely confident in his work of Creation that God was able to take a day off, so should we.

Some pastors are charged with being "control freaks" who must be involved in every act of ministry within their congregations. They are thus impossible to work with, unable to delegate any authority to their church staff, unwilling to give credit to the work of others, resistant to allowing the laity to exercise their baptismally given ministry. Such pastors suffer from a "messiah complex," feeling that if ministry is to occur in the church, it must be done by them or it will not get done. This peculiar brand of clericalism betrays an inadequate theology of resurrection coupled with the inability to observe the Sabbath.

Likewise, the pastor who retired but who would not fully retire, who kept meddling, who kept coming back to his former parish and interfering with the new pastor, was not merely demonstrating poor collegiality, he was also showing a lack of faith in the risen Christ and his Holy Spirit. The church is God's, not ours.

Because none of the habits required of faithful ministerial character come naturally to me, I must pray to God to make me better than I would be if I had not been called to be a pastor. The good news is that, despite myself, even an ordinary person like me—who attends to the habits of submission, study, constancy, humor, and Sabbath—is much better than I could have been if I had been left to my own devices. God has the power to effect that which God promises. God can enable us to embody what we preach. When I was ordained, I not only made promises to God and the church, God made promises to me. In my ordination God promised that if I keep at the practices of ministry, God will bless my ministry, shall grant me fulfillment in it, and shall say, even to an ordinary person like me, "well done thou good and faithful servant."

## MINISTRY IS THE PRESENCE OF CHRIST

Here is one of the sorriest images of the church in the whole New Testament. In fact, it's a picture of the church at its worst, the first miserable little conglomeration ever to take upon itself the name, "church."

> When it was evening on that day, the first day of the week, and the doors of the house where the disciples had met were locked for fear of the Jews, Jesus came and stood among them and said, "Peace be with you." After he said this, he showed them his hands and his side. Then the disciples rejoiced when they saw the Lord. Jesus said to them again, "Peace be with you. As the Father has sent me, so I send you." When he had said this, he breathed on them and said to them, "Receive the Holy Spirit. If you forgive the sins of any, they are forgiven them; if you retain the sins of any, they are retained." (John 20:19-23)

It's the disciples of Jesus, gathered after his resurrection. And look at them! For long, painstaking chapters in John's Gospel, Jesus has been preparing his people for his departure. He has rather redundantly told them to love one another, to be bold, to trust him, to be ready to follow him at all costs.

Somebody wasn't paying attention. Look at them, cowering like frightened rabbits behind bolted doors. They were the ones told to stride into the world, announcing the Easter triumph of God. Look at them hunched down, full of fear, hoping that nobody will find them.

Could this even be called a church? Not only does it have no sanctuary, no pulpit, no choir, and no parking lot, but more significantly it has no plan, no mission, no conviction, and no message. After all of the glory of Easter, the Common Lectionary insists that we read this as the gospel for Low Sunday, just in case someone thinks that the Bible is not realistic and true.

Here is a church with absolutely nothing to commend it as a church except that when it gathered, *the Risen Christ pushed through the locked door, threw back the bolt, and stood among them.*

And maybe that's every church. Left to our own devices, we are nothing more than a huddle of confused, timid, cowering failures to follow Jesus.

Church is a gift. That is why we began this journey into clerical ethics with vocation. We ministers and musicians learn that church is grace. At our chapel we meet every Monday afternoon and evaluate the service from top to bottom. We carefully select every hymn and coordinate each with the texts for the day. Yet we have learned that despite all of our educated planning, worship—real worship—is not of our creation. Ministry is a gift.

When one considers the ministry of the church, soberly, in the reality of Low Sunday, through this many pages of a book on clerical ethics with their necessary catalogue of clerical failure, one is apt to be disheartened. We are, despite our best efforts and because of our worst, not much of a church, not too good at ministry.

But sometimes, by the grace of a living God, the Holy Spirit slips through our closed doors, through our plodding through the Sunday bulletin, and there is worship, and there is church, not of our own creation but as a gift of a God who will not leave us alone. And we take off our shoes in awed wonder that we, despite our faults, have become church.

Toward the end of our *Resident Aliens: Life in the Christian Colony,* Stanley Hauerwas and I noted how there is a great deal of atheism in the contemporary church.[13] We go on with our work as if God were not there. Pastoral counseling degenerates into soothing the anxiety of affluent persons. Preaching becomes the artful evocation of individual emotions. Clergy ethics becomes the skillful management of congregational conflict.

If you want to see us, stripped of our sacred trappings, our pretense peeled away, then look here in this twentieth chapter of John—a pitiful, huddle of timid atheistic souls hanging on to one another behind our locked doors. Without the presence, the presence that makes our human gatherings the church of God, this is us.

And the good news is that it was to *this* church, which was hardly church, that the living, risen Christ came saying "Peace be with you" (John 20:19). Into this frightening void there intruded a voice, a presence.

The voice might have said, "You deserted me when the going got rough," or "Where were you when the soldiers came?" No. He says, "Peace be with you," showing them his pierced hands and feet (cross is still present, even after resurrection). He says again (in case we failed to get the point, knowing how dull we are) "Peace be with you," telling them that he is sending them out into the world. Then he breathes on them, giving them the Holy Spirit, bestowing upon them the awesome power to forgive sins.

Here is the church in its truest sense. Spirit. Mission. Forgiveness. We are church because to us, even to us, he has come and given us his gifts of Spirit, mission, and forgiveness, commissioning us to give them to the whole world in his name.

My first church was in rural Georgia. I was fresh out of seminary, eager to be a good pastor in my first parish. I was in graduate school at the time, commuting out to the hinterland on the weekends. Most Sunday mornings at dawn, it was a tough trip out there from Atlanta. On my first visit, I found a large chain and padlock on the front door, put there, I was told, by the local sheriff. The sheriff? Why? I asked.

"Well, things got out of hand at the board meeting last month, folks started ripping up carpet, dragging out the pews they had given in memory of their mothers. It got bad. The sheriff came out here and put that lock on the door until our new preacher could come and settle things down."

That typified my time at that church. I would drive out each Sunday, praying for a miraculous snowstorm in October that would save me from another Sunday at that so-called church.

I spent a year there that lasted a lifetime. I tried everything. I worked, planned, offered, but the response was always disappointing. The arguments, the pettiness, the fights in the parking lot after the board meeting were more than I could take. It was tough and I was glad to be leaving them behind. "You call yourself a church!" I muttered to myself as my tires kicked gravel up in the parking lot on my last Sunday among them.

A couple of years later, while visiting at Emory, I met a young man who, after introducing himself, told me that he was now serving that church. My heart went out to him. Such a dear young man, and only twenty-three!

"They still remember you out there," he said.

"Yeah," I said glumly, "I'll never forget them either."

"Remarkable bunch of people," he said.

"That's one way of putting it," I said.

"Their ministry to the community has been a wonder," he continued. "That little church is now supporting, in one way or another, more than a dozen of the troubled families around the church. The free day care center is going great. Not too many interracial congregations in this part of the world. What a great place to be for my first church."

I could hardly believe what he was telling me. What happened? I asked.

"I don't know. One Sunday, things just sort of came together. It wasn't anything in particular. It's just that, when the service was done, and we were on our way out, we knew that Jesus loved us and had plans for us. Things fairly much took off after that."

I tell you what I think happened. I think that church got intruded upon. I think someone greater than I knocked the lock off that door, kicked it open and offered them peace, the Holy Spirit, and forgiveness. And now, they are called "church."

Despair over my failures, moral and otherwise, is not permitted a pastor who knows John 20 by heart. Much clergy ethics has its basis here, in our resilient confidence that the same God who raised Jesus from the dead can and will do the same for us as well. Our ethics is not some closed system, not a matter of debating and discerning the rules for right conduct and then following the rules. Our ethics is testimony to the truth that the risen Christ came back to the very followers who had betrayed and forsaken him. Then he forgave them, breathed upon them, and commissioned them to be about his work in the world. His work is the redemption of the world, the recapture of a lost humanity, and the recreation and restoration of Israel. The means of his work, for better or worse, is us. To be enlisted in that mission is a great burden, but on most days, a blessing as well. It is a great blessing to have one's little life caught up in the great doxological crescendo named church, that song sung by the saints throughout the ages, so that we might sing it too today. All Christian ethics, of which clergy ethics is merely a species of a broader genus, has its goal in doxology.

> We thank you, Lord God,
>> for raising up among us faithful servants
>> for the ministry of elders in your Church.
> Clothe them with your righteousness,
>> and grant that we, with them,
>> may glorify you by giving ourselves to others;
> through Jesus Christ our Lord,
> who lives and reigns with you,
> in the unity of the Holy Spirit,
> one God, now and forever. **Amen.**[14]

APPENDIX

# National Capital Presbytery Code of Ethics

for Clergy and Other Church Professionals
*Approved January 24, 1995*

THE PURPOSE OF THESE GUIDELINES: These ethical guidelines for ministerial conduct serve two purposes: as a guide to what is expected professionally of clergy and other church professionals in National Capital Presbytery. They are also to inform the laity what they can expect from clergy and other church professionals (hereafter referred to as "ministers") as defined in G-6.0200 in the Book of Order. It is the expectation of National Capital Presbytery that individual sessions shall adopt similar standards for all of their other employees.

These guidelines do not presume to speak to all areas of ministers' lives. They are minimum expectations and the minister must also be guided by Scripture, personal conscience, the Book of Order, Christian tradition and peer approval. They assume basic honesty and integrity of conduct. Expectations of ministers and styles of behavior change. The ethical behavior of ministers is a topic which should be regularly considered, discussed, and mutually agreed upon by the members of presbytery. This code, however, does articulate certain customs and practices which have been largely accepted within the profession of ministry. They are subject to regular review.

These principles are not designed to be a basis for analysis of the civil liability of those persons guided by them.

## A. SOME FUNDAMENTAL PRINCIPLES

1. In all professional matters, ministers are to maintain practices that give glory to Christ; advance the goals of the Church; and nurture, challenge and protect the welfare of church members, parishioners, clients and the public.

2. Ministers are to act in such a manner as to uphold and enhance the honor, integrity, morality and dignity of the profession.

3. Ministers are to limit their ministries to those positions and responsibilities for which they are qualified.

4. Ministers will conduct all professional matters in a manner which assures confidentiality and avoids conflicts of interest.

5. Ministers will seek to maintain professional competency throughout their careers.

6. In personal as well as professional relationships ministers are to demonstrate honest and sincere motives evidencing respect, honesty and fairness; uphold the peace, unity and purity of the church; and share faith, hope and love with all people.

## B. MINISTERS AS PERSONS

1. MINISTERS BEAR UNIQUE EXPECTATIONS. In considering the ethics particular to ordained ministry, it is well to remember that ministers are expected to live in the same manner of faithfulness, forgiveness and obedience as are all members of Christ's church. While all who follow Christ are subject to the same human weaknesses,

nevertheless, those who are called as ordained servants are set apart with particular expectations.

People expect high standards of ministers. To deny or ignore this is unrealistic and irresponsible. Ministers will show sensible regard for the moral, social and religious standards of the Christian community and the community at large, realizing that any violation on their part may be damaging to their congregants, to colleagues in ministry, to their professions and to the body of Jesus Christ.

2. MINISTERS AND FREEDOM OF CONSCIENCE. Though the Reformed tradition emphasized the freedom of individual conscience, ministers are still subject to the discipline of the church (see Book of Order G-6.0108, G-1.0301, G-1.0302, G-6.0202, G-6.0203). Violations of this code may be cause for disciplinary procedures. (Cf. also Ministers and the Civil Law #4 below.)

Standards for ministerial conduct grow out of a vision of the Christian life and a sense of calling to a particular service. Like other Christians, ministers experience sin, grace, alienation and forgiveness. Along with other Christians, they are expected by the Christian community to witness to the renewal of humanity in Christ by demonstrating in their daily lives love, compassion and respect for other persons; fidelity in marriage; responsibility in parenthood and other family obligations; joy in service; and integrity and trustworthiness in all their dealings with others.

3. THE PASTORAL CARE OF MINISTERS. Ministers also need pastoral care. They should take the initiative in establishing relationships with other ministers, with the Presbytery Executive and with the Committee on Ministry to provide support in difficult times, caring concern, encouragement for Christian growth, and sharing in both successes and failures.

4. MINISTERS AND FEES, HONORARIA AND DIS-
COUNTS. Ministers should ordinarily not require or
solicit fees for pastoral services to families or individuals
within the congregation. Such services include performing baptisms, marriages, funerals and counseling. In
those cases in which an unsolicited gift is given ministers
may use their own best judgment as to what to do with
the gift. All ministers stand ready to render services to
individuals and communities in crisis without regard to
financial remuneration.

While fees for the use of the church facilities are set by
the session, honoraria or fees for the minister's services
to non-members can be set by the minister in consultation with the session. The minister must be aware of and
responsible to civil authorities regarding the possible tax
consequences of receipt of honoraria, gifts, etc.

5. PARTICIPATION IN NON-PARISH ACTIVITIES.
Though ministers are expected to participate in presbytery, ecumenical and other activities beyond the particular
church, it is wise for the minister to discuss the time
involved in such activities with the session. ("Discussion"
does not mean "seek permission," as pastors are expected
to participate in the governing bodies of the church by
virtue of their ordination vows, G-14.0405b.(9).)

If any honoraria are received for duties outside the
particular church (such as speaking, lecturing or teaching), and these duties are carried on during time which
would otherwise be understood as available to the congregation, a common understanding between the minister and the session should be established as to the
disposition of such honoraria. This presupposes agreement between minister and session concerning the limits
of the congregation's claim on the minister's time.
Conversation between ministers and their sessions
should arrive at mutual concurrence as to expectations
regarding the minister's work time and free time.

## C. MINISTERS AND THE PRESBYTERY

1. THE MINISTER AND COLLEAGUES. Whenever a colleague's conduct is believed to be harmful to any individual or group, including that person himself or herself, the concerned person should speak directly to that colleague or consult the presbytery executive or the chairperson of the Committee on Ministry. Anyone registering a concern with regard to the behavior of a colleague will be encouraged to make her or his own identity known.

2. THE MINISTER AND THE NON-MEMBER. Ministers are sometimes called upon to officiate at weddings and funerals for persons who are not members of the congregation. It is appropriate in such situations to ascertain to what particular church these persons belong and to suggest that they procure the services of their own minister.

3. THE MINISTER AND OTHER CHURCHES. Ordinarily ministers should not knowingly call upon members of another church in the community to administer pastoral care unless the initiative and interest shown by such a person requires it as a courtesy. If such a visitation occurs, it is a helpful courtesy to, after obtaining the parishioner's permission, inform the colleague to whose church the person belongs regarding visitation. Marriages, funerals and baptisms are not to be accepted by ministers unless an invitation has been extended by the minister of the church involved.

4. THE MINISTER AND THE MULTIPLE STAFF. All ministers are installed in their positions by action of presbytery and any change in the pastoral relationship must be approved by presbytery. While the minister

serves as head of staff in a congregation and bears the responsibility which this implies, the spirit within the staff should be that of a shared ministry where all bring their particular gifts to the work of ministry. To this end, everyone should be understanding of the mistakes of colleagues and seek to give support and help when needed. Care should be taken to avoid inappropriate criticism, negative suggestions and innuendo. It is not appropriate to attempt to seek to ally other church members and/or co-workers in disagreements. A staff member should not aspire to succeed any other person on staff (Book of Order, G-14.0501.f).

The principles of ethical, healthy staff relationships apply equally to professional, paraprofessional, support staff (secretarial and custodial employees) and volunteers. All staff members are given equal respect without regard to sex, race, ethnic origin, disability, or marital status.

5. THE MINISTER IN AN INTERIM SITUATION. The purpose of an interim minister is to provide pastoral service and to prepare a particular congregation for new pastoral leadership. An interim minister should avoid seeking to mold loyalties to the interim minister and should instead direct a congregation's attention to the new challenges in mission and ministry that manifest themselves in a period of transition to new pastoral leadership. An interim minister should make clear and without ambiguity that presbytery takes very seriously the Book of Order G-14.0513b, namely that "a minister may not be called to be the next installed minister or associate minister of a church served as interim minister."

Under no circumstances should an interim minister become involved in the work of the pastor nominating committee beyond preparation of the Church Information Form. Presbytery representatives should make this policy clear to the congregation at the time the congregation elects a pastor nominating committee.

6. THE MINISTER AND THE SUCCESSOR. When a minister accepts another call, the minister should exercise due care not to influence directly or indirectly the policies of the successor. Frequent visits to one's former parish should be avoided. Even when occasional visits occur, it is a courtesy to pay one's respects to one's successor and to inform the successor about the nature and purpose of the visit. During the period of temporary supply or interim, the former minister should avoid performing ministerial services (weddings, funerals, baptisms, etc). Moreover, even when a successor issues an invitation to a former minister to assist or take part in a ministerial function, it is a wise idea for the former minister to take the initiative in a candid discussion with the successor about the propriety of such functioning and the possible harmful effects of the life of the congregation in terms of its new ministry. One reasonable and workable rule of thumb is for a former minister to make clear to former parishioners that the former minister would accept an invitation of the present minister only to assist the present minister in a ministerial function. In any case, regarding all such situations, the former minister and the present minister should seek the advice and approval of the current session of the church. If misunderstandings arise in these areas, it is appropriate for the former minister and the present minister to seek the counsel of presbytery's Committee on Ministry. The Book of Order, G-14.0606 states: "Former ministers, associate ministers, and assistant ministers may officiate at services for members of a particular church, or at services within its properties, only upon invitation from the moderator of the session, or in the case of the inability to contact the moderator, from the clerk of session."

7. THE MINISTER AND THE PREDECESSOR. If the former minister or retired minister bears primary responsibility for making clear that the ministry in a given location should be directed to the future rather than to the past, it is the primary responsibility of the successor or the currently installed minister to show respect and gratitude for the heritage of that church and for the positive work of the predecessor. Ordinarily it is wise for the successor to take the initiative in making contact with a predecessor to discuss the mission and work of the church. There may be occasions when it is appropriate to invite a predecessor to return to the church for a visit, possibly to celebrate a special occasion or event or, if deemed appropriate by all concerned, to assist in a ministerial function.

8. THE MINISTER AND RETIREMENT. The above discussions (#s 6 & 7) are relevant for the retired minister, but some additional matters also require comment. Sometimes a retired minister remains within the boundaries of presbytery and sometimes within proximity to a former church. This can create problems both for the successor and for the retired minister. This should be a matter for serious discussion by the session of the local church and presbytery's Committee on Ministry. Perhaps most important is for all concerned to recognize some fundamental professional priorities, namely: (a) that the local church and its new ministry should be uppermost in everybody's mind; (b) that the new ministry will probably develop new directions and should be encouraged in freedom to do so; (c) that there will be a natural tendency for some in the church to resist change and that it is very important for the successor and the retired minister to deal with this resistance by reiterating with love and understanding that the mission of the church should be oriented to the future rather than the past.

The retired minister or staff person who still remains within the bounds of presbytery or in proximity to the local church bears primary responsibility for making these priorities known. Moreover, the retired minister should make it entirely clear that "retired" means "withdrawn from active service," at least in that location. There may naturally be misunderstandings about these matters, and there may be occasions when the line between "old friend" and "parishioner" will be unclear. In all such cases of ambiguity, again it is the retired minister who bears primary responsibility for making clear what "retired" means.

One obvious way to ease the pain in such situations is for the retired minister and the family involved to relocate to a residence some distance away from the former parish and to become active in another church in a non-professional role; economically, however, moving is not always feasible. Another way to deal with such situations is for the retired minister to have candid conversation with the installed minister regarding their mutual feelings in terms of collegial interaction. Where there is a difference of opinion, the retired minister should defer to the installed minister with respect to collegiality in that location. In the case of lack of agreement or uncertainty, it is appropriate for either minister to seek the guidance of the Committee on Ministry.

9. "TEACHERS, CHAPLAINS, AND OTHERS" (G-6.0203). All ministers who fall into the category of the Book of Order's listing of "others" are expected to be active in the life of a particular congregation while respecting the position of installed ministers regarding all ministerial functions within the community. Counselors should also refer to their own code of ethics.

Ministers may administer the sacraments only at the request of the minister or session concerned, or by permission of the presbytery.

## D. ETHICAL ISSUES OF PARTICULAR CONCERN

1. MINISTERS AND CONFIDENTIALITY. Ministers shall not disclose confidences to anyone except when:

a. required to do so by law [Most states will not require this].

b. disclosure is consented to by the person communicating confidences, which consent is normally given in writing.

c. disclosure is necessary to prevent the person from harming himself or herself or others. Harmful behavior is that which is a violation of law or poses a threat to the physical well-being of the self or others.

d. disclosure is necessary to defend a minister against claims made by a person who asserts that particular communications related to the claim were made in confidence.

2. MINISTERS AND SPECIAL PRIVILEGES. Ministers, as servants of the Servant of God, need to be sensitive to the danger of any use of the authority of the pastoral office for personal benefit. Boundaries should be set, in consultation between the minister, the session and the Committee on Ministry to determine how much and in what manner a minister may promote among the members of the congregation any of the minister's private business endeavors, tours or products. The same consultation should occur concerning the minister's private use of church resources, business machines, secretarial time, etc.

3. BUSINESS AND FINANCE. The minister's integrity in personal business and financial dealings is also an ethical concern. Ministers are expected to conduct their

financial affairs with the utmost integrity. Many ministers manage discretionary funds on behalf of the congregation. It is suggested that wherever possible the minister identify someone in the congregation or presbytery to audit the use of this money. This suggestion is made to protect the minister both from the temptation to use the funds unwisely and from rumors in the congregation about his/her misuse of the funds.

Ministers are not to solicit clergy discounts for merchandise or services rendered them.

4. THE MINISTER AND THE CIVIL LAW. The minister shall him/herself obey the civil law and insist leaders and members of his/her congregation do likewise. This includes, but is not limited to, matters related to taxes, copyrights, insurance, marriages, and the keeping of records.

There may be times when the minister affirms the necessity of civil disobedience for moral reasons. Whether this is done alone or in conjunction with others (including officers and members of the congregation), it shall be done openly and with a willingness to accept the consequences of the law. However, in such cases no moral justification for violence against another person or property is acceptable.

5. PREACHING AND WRITING. The minister's public preaching, teaching and writing shall always be her or his own work with appropriate academic acknowledgment. In sermons this includes the exegetical work, the organization and the words of the sermon, and the use of examples and illustrations.

6. LANGUAGE AND BEHAVIOR. The minister shall recognize her or his unique position in the eyes of the congregation. It is a position of trust. This position shall

not be abused through misuse of ministerial authority. In visits, counseling sessions, or other contacts with members of the congregation, the minister shall maintain strict decorum. Ministers shall not treat persons arbitrarily based on their gender, race, nationality, age, physical, emotional or mental condition, sexual orientation, or economic condition.

Ministers shall avoid discriminatory or harassing treatment of any person or group. Ministerial language shall not include slurs or other verbal conduct relating to gender, race, etc., which has the purpose or effect of creating an intimidating, hostile, or offensive environment. Sexual harassment shall not take place. This includes but is not limited to verbal or non-verbal behavior such as sexist remarks, demeaning statements relating to gender, pressure for sexual activity and threats of punishment or promises of rewards for sexual behavior.

Sexual abuse of or misconduct with a congregational member shall be understood as strictly forbidden. The professional has the responsibility to set the boundaries and to maintain them.

Due to the issues of power and trust involved, it is recommended that single pastors or professional church workers not date members of their congregations. The same is true for presbytery staff members regarding the members of committees or other groups they staff.

These provisions shall include ministers of presbytery who are involved as teachers, counselors, or supervisors in programs which train for special work in ministry, e.g., Clinical Pastoral Education or Spiritual Development.

As professionals, ministers are aware of the variation in spiritual and psychological dynamics at work in a person. Where the minister himself or herself feels compulsions to behavior which is either criminal or unethical he or she will seek immediate help from an appropriate counselor. This standard shall apply to those caught in substance, drug, or alcohol abuse or addiction. If therapy or counseling seems to be unfruitful the minister shall lay aside the office of ministry.

7. THE MINISTER AND RUMORS. The minister may find her/himself the subject of rumors in the congregation or community. Response to these shall be carefully considered. No action including verbal response shall be taken without consultation with the Session or an appropriate committee of a higher governing body. The goal of whatever action taken shall be to end such rumors; hostile action toward the bearer of such rumors endangers the life of the congregation as well as the spiritual or emotional health of the perpetrator. It is not acceptable.

## E. CIRCULATION OF ETHICAL STANDARDS

National Capital Presbytery will circulate this code of ethics among its member churches and minister members. Each minister shall submit a signed statement certifying he/she has read the code of ethics, is aware of the standards of the presbytery, and will make a sincere, good faith effort to abide with both the spirit and the letter of this code of ethics.

## F. ETHICAL COUNSELORS

National Capital Presbytery will appoint a number of its members to serve as counselors in understanding and fulfilling these standards. These counselors will not be members of the presbytery's staff.

## G. VIOLATIONS AND SANCTIONS

The presbytery considers that fidelity to these standards enhances the peace, unity, and purity of the church. Violations of these standards may be viewed as a breaking of ordination vows and subject to the disciplinary processes of the <u>Book of Order</u> of the Presbyterian Church in the United States of America.

## H. CANDIDATES AND INQUIRERS

The Committee on Preparation for Ministry shall circulate these standards to its inquirers and candidates for the ministry. It shall make clear that these standards apply also to those under its supervision.

## I. CONCLUSION AND RATIONALE

Central to the vocation of Minister of Word and Sacrament is leadership of the people of God in a peculiarly Christian lifestyle which has at its core the embodiment of Jesus' words in John 15:12. "This is my commandment, that you love one another as I have loved you."

These ethical standards are an attempt, not at setting legalistic limitations but rather guiding us all in showing the kind of love for each other that Christ has shown. So may all be encouraged to live in such a manner as to promote the health and growth of the Church, and give glory to God in Jesus Christ.

References: American Association of Pastoral Counselors Code of Ethics and Procedures, April 28, 1994

<u>National Capital Presbytery's Sexual Misconduct Policy and Procedures</u>

# Notes

## INTRODUCTION

1. *The United Methodist Book of Worship* (Nashville: The United Methodist Publishing House, 1992), 677.

2. Richard Hays stresses the dynamic way in which the New Testament does ethics, moving from narrative to normative ethics in *The Moral Vision of the New Testament: Community, Cross, New Creation, A Contemporary Introduction to New Testament Ethics* (San Francisco: HarperSanFrancisco, 1996), p. 295.

3. *The Peaceable Kingdom: A Primer in Christian Ethics* (Notre Dame, Ind.: University of Notre Dame Press, 1983), p. 70.

4. Thanks to my colleague in ethics, Harmon L. Smith, for helping me sort out some of this theoretical basis for my discussion of ethics. I also wish to thank my colleagues Richard B. Hays and Stanley M. Hauerwas, as well as my friends in campus ministry at Duke University for their help and critique of my work on this book.

5. *The Preaching of Chrysostom* Jaroslav Pelikan, ed., (Philadelphia: Fortress, 1967), p. 24.

6. In my own church family, the classic text on ministerial ethics, at least for the past three generations, has been Bishop Nolan B. Harmon's, *Ministerial Ethics and Etiquette* (Nashville: Abingdon, 1928; latest revision in 1987). Today, this good book is at times laughably dated. It is best read as a compendium of advice to Protestant pastors by a master pastor. The great virtue of the book is Harmon's high regard for the ministerial calling. All of his advice is based upon the

conviction that there can be no higher vocation than that of a pastor. Futhermore, Harmon's stress on ministerial etiquette, while somewhat quaint, also has much to commend it. Our ethics is best known in the concrete, specific practices in which we engage.

My work in ethics began with my book, *The Service of God: How Worship and Ethics Are Related* (Nashville: Abingdon, 1983). While this book will not venture into much specific advice on daily ministerial practice, I hope that it provides a theological basis for such consideration by pastors themselves.

# CHAPTER ONE: VOCATION

1. Aristotle made the first ethical question, the prior question before any other questions, "What is the proper function of humanity?" In modernity, after Kant, there was an attempt to do ethics without inquiry into proper ends. Ethics became a matter of quandaries about what to do in certain situations rather than, as Aristotle contended, an inquiry into who human beings ought to be in order to be most properly human.

This book, you will note, is more in line with Aristotelian "virtue ethics" than situational, contextual, principled, or decision ethics. See Wendell Berry's delightful reworking of this theme in his aptly entitled, *What Are People For?* (New York: North Point Press, 1990).

Walter E. Wiest and Elwyn A. Smith (*Ethics in Ministry* [Minneapolis: Fortress, 1990]) show the fruitfulness and the problems involved in approaching clergy ethics as dilemmas and situations. I find that they give too little weight to the peculiar shape of specifically *Christian* ethics, taking too many of their cues from professional ethics in general.

2. One can understand the reluctance of some feminist commentators to embrace these servant metaphors as being descriptive of Christian ministry. In our culture and in the church, women have been relegated to servile, domestic roles. Thus Elisabeth Schüssler Fiorenza says that, "at the heart of the spiritual feminist quest is the quest for women's power, freedom, and independence. Is it possible to read the Bible in such a way that it becomes a historical source and theological symbol for such power, independence, and freedom?" (*In Memory of Her: A Feminist Theological Reconstruction of Christian Origins* [New York: Crossroad, 1983], pp. 18-19.) While she presents her critique as countercultural, it is not. Her language here, so thoroughly modernist, individual, and capitalist, is a helpful illustration that, while the images of ministry as *diakonia* must be carefully and

critically interpreted, they are appropriately countercultural for a community whose originator placed his gathered people at great odds with the dominant metaphors for human fulfillment like "power, independence, and freedom." See also Edward C. Zaragoza, *No Longer Servants, but Friends: A Theology of Ordained Ministry* (Nashville: Abingdon, 1999) for a critique of the servant image of ministry.

3. John Chrysostom, *Treatise Concerning the Christian Priesthood,* Books 1–5, trans. W. R. W. Stephens, vol. 9, *A Select Library of Nicene and Post-Nicene Fathers of the Christian Church,* ed. Philip Schaff (New York: The Christian Literature Co., 1889).

4. Ibid., p. 241.

5. James P. Wind, J. Russell Burck, Paul F. Camenisch, and Dennis P. McCann, eds. (Louisville: Westminster/John Knox, 1991).

6. Stanley Hauerwas and I have attempted to think through some of these issues in our article, "Ministry As More Than a Helping Profession," *The Christian Century* (March 15, 1989), pp. 282-84.

7. Robert W. Jenson, "Marriage and Ministry," *Lutheran Forum 31* (Winter 1997), pp. 20-21.

8. *The United Methodist Book of Worship* (Nashville: The United Methodist Publishing House, 1992), pp. 688-89.

## CHAPTER TWO: THE CHARACTER OF CLERGY

1. Richard John Neuhaus, *Freedom for Ministry* (San Francisco: Harper & Row, 1979), p. xi.

2. Brooks Hollifield tells the story of the history of pastoral care in America as a long story of the clergy being subsumed into one culturally dominant image of success after another in *A History of Pastoral Care in America: From Salvation to Self-Realization* (Nashville: Abingdon, 1983).

3. Gaylord Noyce (*Pastoral Ethics: Professional Responsibilities of the Clergy* [Nashville: Abingdon, 1988]) makes a valiant effort to make pastoral ethics professional. In my judgment, Noyce demonstrates the problems involved in attempting to do clergy ethics with an inadequate theological basis.

Dennis M. Campbell also attempted to salvage the professional image for ministry in his *Doctors, Lawyers, Ministers: Christian Ethics in Professional Practice* (Nashville: Abingdon, 1982).

4. See Stanley M. Hauerwas, "Clerical Character," in *Christian Existence Today: Essays on Church, World, and Living in Between* (Durham, N.C.: Labyrinth Press, 1988), p. 141.

The fruitfulness of character ethics can be seen in *Practice What You Preach: Virtues, Ethics, and Power in the Lives of Pastoral Ministers and Their Congregations* by James F. Keenan, S.J. and Joseph Kotva Jr. ([Franklin, Wisc.: Sheed & Ward], 1999). In her essay, "Virtual Ethics and the Sexual Formation of Clergy," Sondra Ely Wheeler praises character and virtue ethics as those "skills, dispositions, and habits that enable us to behave rightly under pressure, and with how they are to be cultivated." Furthermore, Wheeler says that virtue ethics give us "a language for and a description of those central features of character that we need . . . the four cardinal virtues of prudence, temperance, justice, and fortitude" (p. 102). She notes the paradoxical classical insight that "you cannot act virtuously without possessing virtue, and you cannot develop virtue without acting virtuously," (p. 103) thus stressing ethics as a matter of practices, not simply a set of ideas. I agree with Wheeler when she also asserts that far too many accounts of clergy ethics are reactive, reacting to cases of sexual misconduct when our time might be well spent in being proactive, troubling ourselves over what sorts of persons ought to be, and might be sustained as, clergy. This suggests to me that the ethical trouble begins early, at least in seminary, when seminary education is conceived of as skills and insights to be acquired by the developing clergyperson rather than as practices to be assumed and cultivated.

5. Richard Lischer shows how important was the issue of character in past discussions of preaching in Section Two of his *Theories of Preaching* (Durham, N.C.: Labyrinth Press, 1987).

6. Augustine, *Great Books of the Western World,* vol. 18, ed. Robert Hutchins and Mortimer Adler (Chicago: W. Benton, 1952), p. 696.

7. William F. May says, "One test of character and virtue is what a person does when no one else is watching." "Professional Ethics: Setting, Terrain, and Teacher," in Daniel Callahan and Sissel Bok, eds., *Ethics Teaching in Higher Education* (New York: Plenum, 1980), p. 231.

8. Gregory of Nyssa, *On the Baptism of Christ,* quoted in H. Richard Niebuhr and Daniel D. Williams, *The Ministry in Historical Perspectives* (New York: Harper & Brothers, 1956), p. 75.

9. Chrysostom, *Treatise Concerning the Christian Priesthood,* Book Two, p. 110.

10. If we are to have a clergy code of conduct, I very much like the one proposed by Richard M. Gula, S.S. in *Ethics In Pastoral Ministry* ([New York: Paulist, 1996], pp. 149-52).

11. See Philip K. Howard, *The Death of Common Sense: How Law Is Suffocating America* (New York: Random House, 1994).

12. Chrysostom, *Treatise Concerning the Christian Priesthood,* Book Four, p. 241.

13. Ibid., p. 244.

14. J. Miller et al., ed., *Readings in Medieval Rhetoric* (Bloomington: Indiana University Press, 1973), p. 168.

15. St. Athanasius, *On the Incarnation* (New York: Macmillan, 1946), p. 90. In his now classic essay, Nicholas Lash says that "the fundamental form of the Christian interpretation of scripture is the life, activity, and organization of the believing community" (*Theology on the Way to Emmaus* [London, SCM, 1986], p. 42).

16. Thomas Benson and Michael Prosser, ed., *Readings in Classical Rhetoric* (Bloomington: Indiana University Press, 1969), p. 136.

17. Quoted in *The Preaching of John Henry Newman*, ed. W.D. White (Philadelphia: Fortress, 1969), p. 28.

18. Hauerwas, "Clerical Character," p. 144.

19. So Hauerwas says that, "our seminaries have no more important function—than to direct those preparing for and in the ministry to reflect on those lives that have honored their calling as ministers." See "Clerical Character," p. 145. For this reason I enjoy having seminarians read autobiographies and biographies of ministers.

20. David Bartlett, *Ministry in the New Testament* (Philadelphia: Fortress, 1993), p. 183.

21. Chrysostom, *Treatise Concerning the Christian Priesthood*, Book Three, p. 198.

22. Ibid.

23. All Kierkegaard quotes are from *Provocations: Spiritual Writings of Kierkegaard*, ed. and comp. Charles E. Moore (Farmington, Pa.: The Plough Publishing House, 1999), pp. 350-58.

24. Aristotle, *Nichomachean Ethics*, II, 1.

25. Richard B. Hays discusses and defends these three focal images in *The Moral Vision of the New Testament* (San Francisco: HarperSanFrancisco, 1996), pp. 196-98. I would have preferred that Hays had simply said "church" when he talks about "community," but of course he means church. Hays says that he is troubled that the term "church" could be "misunderstood in terms of an institutional hierarchy." I think this a bit squeamish of him since I cannot envision any Christian embodiment without institution and without hierarchy.

Hays is fully aware of the perils of abstracting overarching themes out of the complex New Testament narrative, yet I feel that he demonstrates the validity of his use of these three. Hays is critical (pp. 253-66) of Hauerwas's character ethics program primarily because Hays thinks Hauerwas is not a careful, critical interpreter of Scripture. He also finds that Hauerwas neglects, in his stress upon communitarian interpretation of Scripture, the Protestant stress upon the way that Scripture not only arises out of and confirms the church, but is also the church's most severe critic. Nevertheless, Hays would certainly support Hauerwas's ecclesial stress (it resembles Hays's "community" criterion) and surely Hauerwas would be positive about Hays's three focal images, though I suspect Hauerwas would like to add to them peaceableness and nonviolence.

While the extensive study of desirable characteristics of ministers (conducted by Association of Theological Schools in the United States and Canada) highlighted certain clerical virtues (being of service without regard for public recognition, integrity, or generosity), it lacked theological rationale. Thus one wondered if the character traits desired of clergy were merely a commentary upon public taste rather than traits that specifically arose out of Christian commitments. See Daniel O. Aleshire, "ATS Profiles of Ministry Project," in Richard Hunt, John E. Hinkle, and H. Newton Malony, ed., *Clergy Assessment and Career Development* (Nashville: Abingdon, 1990), especially pp. 97-103.

I decided to use Hays's three focal images after reading Richard Bondi, *Leading God's People: Ethics for the Practice of Ministry* (Nashville: Abingdon, 1989). In many ways, Bondi's is a sensitive, eloquent investigation of pastoral ethics, particularly noteworthy for its stress upon the narrative formation of pastors. Yet I felt that his exposition lacked biblical, christological substance. I hope that Hays's images will give my book that specificity and substance.

26. Hays, *Moral Vision*, p. 197.

27. William H. Willimon, *Worship As Pastoral Care* (Nashville: Abingdon Press, 1979), pp. 198-218.

28. Hays, *Moral Vision*, p. 197.

29. Paul was certainly unashamed to invoke his parental status over the congregation at Corinth to motivate them to do what he desired. See 1 Corinthians 4:14-17.

## CHAPTER THREE: THE PASTOR IN COMMUNITY

1. Paradoxically, the election of a particular people, Israel and the church, is God's way of being universal. Bishop Lesslie Newbigin's universal missionary theology was based upon his conviction that, "the Bible seems to teach consistently that God's gift of salvation (which is certainly intended for all) works by the principle of election, one being chosen to be the means of God's saving grace to others." Cited in George R. Hunsberger, *Bearing the Witness of the Spirit: Lesslie Newbigin's Theology of Cultural Plurality* (Grand Rapids: Eerdmans, 1998), p. 46.

2. As Stanley Hauerwas stresses, the gospel is a narrative means of

forming characters as Christians in community. As people so formed, Christians are a political alternative to all other means of organizing people (i.e., the modern nation) and are a witness to the power of the gospel to form an alternative people. See *A Community of Character: Toward a Constructive Christian Social Ethic* (Notre Dame: University of Notre Dame Press, 1981).

3. This is what I interpret John Howard Yoder to mean when he says that, "the Church precedes the world epistemologically." As quoted by Hays, *The Moral Vision of the New Testament: Community, Cross, New Creation, A Contemporary Introduction to New Testament Ethics* (San Francisco: HarperSanFrancisco, 1996), p. 252.

4. Walter Brueggemann, *The Covenanted Self: Explorations of Law and Covenant* (Minneapolis: Fortress, 1999), p. 10.

5. The most thorough investigation of the issue of clergy confidentiality is William W. Rankin's, *Confidentiality and Clergy: Churches, Ethics and the Law* (Harrisburg, Pa.: Morehouse, 1990) though I find Rankin leaning too heavily upon legal rather than theological criteria for confidentiality. He does give some excellent guidance to clergy who are faced with conflicts related to confidentiality, particularly in situations where there is abuse or possible criminal behavior. Even after his painstaking examination of the details of conflicts over confidentiality, I was pleased to read his conclusion that when all is said and done in matters as complex as confidentiality, what we most require are "basically intelligent, caring, respectful, and considerate" people, in short, persons of virtue and character. I agree.

On confidentiality, see also Richard M. Gula, S.S., *Ethics in Pastoral Ministry* (New York: Paulist, 1996), chapter 6.

6. See Randy Frame, "Christian Children's Fund Practices Questioned," *Christianity Today*, Nov. 14, 1994, p. 71.

7. The self-pity of clergy can be a great hindrance to clear thinking. The "stones" being cast are not from a group of privileged men toward a defenseless woman with death as a possible result. Rather, the matter under discussion was the church's calling to account a powerful person who had taken advantage of the powerlessness of another.

8. Neil and Thea Ormerod's, *When Ministers Sin* (Alexandria, N.S.W., Australia: Millennium Books, 1995) is a fine treatment of the ways in which clergy sexual abuse is related to the complex interplay of ministerial power and vulnerability.

9. I believe that Marie M. Fortune's, *Is Nothing Sacred: When Sex Invades the Pastoral Relationship* (San Francisco: HarperSanFrancisco, 1992) is a wonderful treatment of this issue, particularly as a congregational tragedy. I especially like the way that Fortune, while in no way excusing the clergy from responsibility, stresses steps that a congregation can take

to protect itself from and to prepare itself for sexually abusing clergy. See also Jan Winebrenner and Debra Frazier, *When a Leader Falls: What Happens to Everyone Else?* (Minneapolis: Bethany House, 1993).

10. Rebekah Miles, "Keeping Watch Over the Shepherds by Day and Night," *Circuit Rider,* May/June 1999, pp. 14-15.

11. Alasdair MacIntyre, *After Virtue,* 2nd ed. (Notre Dame, Ind.: University of Notre Dame Press, 1984), p. 151.

12. As reported in a number of the essays in Nancy Myer Hopkins, ed., *Clergy Sexual Misconduct: A Systems Perspective* (Washington, D.C.: The Alban Institute, 1993).

13. Martha C. Nussbaum, *The Fragility of Goodness: Luck and Ethics in Greek Tragedy and Philosophy* (Cambridge: Cambridge University Press, 1986). See also Paul J. Wadell, *Friendship and the Moral Life* (Notre Dame, Ind.: University of Notre Dame Press, 1989).

14. After surveying a number of contemporary novels on ministry, James P. Wind notes that nearly all of them appear to regard the church as a negative resource for pastors in trouble. Always, in these novels the church "appears as problem, burden, inhibitor, complicator." ("Clergy Ethics in Modern Fiction," in *Clergy Ethics in a Changing Society,* ed., James P. Wind, J. Russell Burck, Paul F. Camenisch, and Dennis P. McCann [Louisville: Westminster/John Knox, 1991], pp. 99-113).

15. Stanley Hauerwas, *Unleashing the Scriptures: Freeing the Bible from Captivity to America* (Nashville: Abingdon, 1993), p. 64.

16. John Howard Yoder, *The Priestly Kingdom: Social Ethics As Gospel* (Notre Dame, Ind.: University of Notre Dame Press, 1984), p. 43.

17. Stanley M. Hauerwas, "Clerical Character," in *Christian Existence Today: Essays on Church, World, and Living in Between* (Durham, N.C.: Labyrinth Press, 1988), p. 144.

18. I have long been fascinated by the story of the lynching of Willie Earle, having used it as a basis for my reflection in my earlier *Sighing for Eden: Sin, Evil, and the Christian Faith* (Nashville: Abingdon, 1985). My information on Hawley Lynn's sermon on the lynching is from Will Gravely, " '... A Man Lynched in Inhuman Lawlessness': South Carolina Methodist Hawley Lynn Condemns the Killing of Willie Earle (1947)," *Methodist History,* January 1997, vol. XXXV, Number 2, pp. 71-80.

## CHAPTER FOUR: CROSSBEARING AND THE CLERGY

1. Dietrich Bonhoeffer, *The Cost of Discipleship,* trans. R. H. Fuller (New York: Macmillan, 1949), p. 38.

2. *A History of Pastoral Care in America: From Salvation to Self-Realization* (Nashville: Abingdon, 1983).

3. Desiderius Erasmus, *The Praise of Folly*, trans. Hoyt Hopewell Hudson (New York: Modern Library, 1941), p. 111.

4. Søren Kierkegaard, *Provocations: Spiritual Writings of Kierkegaard*, ed. Charles E. Moore (Farmington, Pa.: The Plough Publishing House, 1999), pp. 350-58.

5. Anson Shupe, ed., *Wolves Within the Fold* (New Brunswick, N.J.: Rutgers University Press, 1998) has some excellent and deeply disturbing data on and interpretation of financial malfeasance among the clergy.

6. Richard John Neuhaus, *Freedom for Ministry* (San Francisco: Harper & Row, 1979), pp. 191-92.

7. Kierkegaard, *Provocations*, pp. 350-58.

8. Jack L. Sammons Jr., "Rebellious Ethics and Albert Speer," in *Against the Grain: New Approaches to Professional Ethics* (Valley Forge, Pa.: Trinity, 1993), pp. 123-60.

Karen Lebacqz warns of the dangers of thoughtlessly merging the "personal" with the "professional." Her views are counter to those of Sammons, who stresses the positive value of our role and the impossibility of sorting out what is "personal" and what is "professional." See Karen Lebacqz, *Professional Ethics: Power and Paradox* (Nashville: Abingdon, 1985), p. 38. In addition, Lebacqz warns that "total identification with roles can be dangerous when it comes to ethics. The person may lose his or her ability to question the normal expectations that go with the role. . . . Indeed, we get our caricatures of professional groups—the stealthy lawyer, the overly pious minister—from taking to extremes the normal role morality of those groups" (p. 35).

9. I found Lebacqz's, *Professional Ethics* particularly astute in its analysis of the intricacies of pastoral power.

10. Martin Marty, "Clergy Ethics in America: The Ministers on Their Own," in *Clergy Ethics* (Louisville: Westminster/John Knox, 1991), pp. 23-36.

11. Marty, *Clergy Ethics*, p. 29.

12. Ibid.

13. Chrysostom, *Treatise Concerning the Christian Priesthood*, Book One, pp. 58-59.

14. Martin Luther, "A Mighty Fortress Is Our God," no. 110, *The United Methodist Hymnal* (Nashville: The United Methodist Publishing House).

15. Richard B. Hays, *The Moral Vision of the New Testament: Community, Cross, New Creation* (San Francisco: HarperSanFrancisco, 1996), p. 205.

16. Samuel K. Roberts ("Virtue Ethics and the Problem of African American Clergy Ethics in the Culture of Deference," in *Practice What*

*You Preach: Virtues, Ethics, and Power in the Lives of Pastoral Ministers and Their Congregations,* ed. James F. Keenan and Joseph Kotva [Kansas City, Mo.: Sheed and Ward, 1999], pp. 128-38) speaks of African American clergy working in a "culture of deference" in which the African American church accords "the preacher relatively higher normative status and authority than other professionals." Roberts notes the ways in which this deference can lead to lack of accountability and a sense that clergy are above the limits of basic morality.

17. Thomas G. Long, "Shepherds, Strangers, and Thieves," *Pulpit Resource* (April 25, 1999), vol. 27, no. 2, p. 22, quoting Jonathan Kozol, *Amazing Grace* (New York: HarperPerennial, 1996).

18. Hauerwas, "Clerical Character," p. 143.

19. Hays, *Moral Vision,* pp. 3-4.

20. John Howard Yoder, *The Politics of Jesus* (Grand Rapids: Eerdmans, 1994), p. 53.

## CHAPTER FIVE: NEW CREATION

1. The accounts of Paul's "conversion" are more properly interpreted as stories of vocation rather than conversion. To be called, according to Paul, is to be changed, transformed, and converted. The point seems important in the context of this book's thesis. See William H. Willimon, *Acts: Interpretation* (Atlanta: John Knox, 1988), pp. 73-79.

2. Allan Verhey, *The Great Reversal: Ethics and the New Testament* (Grand Rapids: Eerdmans, 1984), pp. 181-83.

3. Richard B. Hays, *The Moral Vision of the New Testament: Community, Cross, New Creation, A Contemporary Introduction to New Testament Ethics* (San Francisco: HarperSanFrancisco, 1996), p. 24.

4. I have always wondered whether or not Jesus' words that he would always be with us, even to the end of the world, are to be interpreted as a promise or a threat. That the crucified one whom we, his disciples, betrayed, is also the resurrected one who will stick with us even to the end of the age seems to me to have more than a measure of threat. I interpret these words here, in the light of new creation, as a promise.

5. "Finally we must ask of those in ministry whether they are capable of joy; if they are not they lack a character sufficient to their calling. For a person incapable of joy will lack the humor necessary for the self-knowledge that that character requires" (Hauerwas, "Clerical Character," p. 143).

6. John Dominic Crossan, *The Dark Interval: Towards a Theology of Story* (Santa Rosa, Calif.: Polebridge Press, 1994).

7. Although his book is not nearly as funny as it ought to be, Paul Duke's *Irony in the Fourth Gospel* (Atlanta: John Knox Press, 1985) cultivates an appreciation for the potential humor in John's Gospel. Richard Hays stresses the irony in Mark, a Gospel that, in Hays's estimation, teaches disciples "not to take ourselves too seriously" and to be "self-critical and receptive to unexpected manifestations of God's love and power" (Hays, *Moral Vision*, p. 90).

8. William Stringfellow, *Count It All Joy: Reflections on Faith, Doubt, and Temptation Seen Through the Letter of James* (Grand Rapids: Eerdmans, 1967), p. 20.

Bill Wylie Kellermann has edited a wonderful volume of William Stringfellow's writings aptly titled *A Keeper of the Word* (Grand Rapids: Eerdmans, 1994).

9. J. F. Powers, *Wheat That Springeth Green* (New York: Knopf, 1988), p. 175.

10. A colleague told me about an old priest he once met at a party. The priest told him he had just celebrated his fiftieth anniversary of ordination and proceeded to tell him about his life.

"I preached bad news for the first twenty-five years," he said. "I did what I thought I was supposed to do. I made life difficult for my congregation. I was really hard on them. Then I became afflicted with a disease that took my sight and made it impossible for me to continue as a pastor. I moved to an apartment and could no longer drive. Riding around on busses and walking to where I had to go, I became acquainted with street people, prostitutes and the like. They taught me about life. I learned to preach the good news, which I have done for the last twenty-five years of my priesthood.

"I guess learning to preach the good news is a process that we learn as we struggle with life. Sometimes we make big mistakes along the way. We lose our sense of humor and take ourselves too seriously—then get into trouble. There is room for a repentant preacher."

11. Karl Barth, *Church Dogmatics*, vol. 3, part 4, trans. A. T. MacKay et al. (Edinburgh: T & T Clark, 1961), p. 53.

12. Ibid., p. 50. See also Stanley M. Hauerwas and William H. Willimon, *The Truth About God: The Ten Commandments in Christian Life* (Nashville: Abingdon, 1999), chapter 3.

13. (Nashville: Abingdon, 1989).

14. Prayer at the end of The Order for the Ordination of Elders, *The United Methodist Book of Worship* (Nashville: The United Methodist Publishing House, 1992), p. 682.

# Subject Index

# Scripture Index